MW00654281

THE ORVIS POCKET GUIDE TO
Nymphing Techniques

Books by Tom Rosenbauer

The Orvis Fly-Fishing Guide
The Orvis Guide to Reading Trout Streams
The Orvis Guide to Prospecting for Trout
Casting Illusions
*The Orvis Streamside Guide to Trout Foods and
    Their Imitations*
*The Orvis Streamside Guide to Approach and
    Presentation*
The Orvis Fly-Fishing Manual
The Orvis Fly-Tying Guide

THE ORVIS POCKET GUIDE TO NYMPHING TECHNIQUES

Naturals and Imitations * Tackle * Fishing With and Without Indicators * Reading Water * Matching Strategies to the Season * and Much More

Tom Rosenbauer

The Lyons Press
Guilford, Connecticut
An imprint of The Globe Pequot Press

Copyright © 2002 by Tom Rosenbauer

Illustrations by Rod Walinchus

All rights reserved. No part of this book may be reproduced or transmitted in any form by any means, electronic or mechanical, including photocopying and recording, or by any information storage and retrieval system, except as may be expressly permitted by the 1976 Copyright Act or in writing from the publisher. Requests for permission should be addressed to The Globe Pequot Press, P.O. Box 480, Guilford, CT 06437.

The Lyons Press is an imprint of The Globe Pequot Press.

Printed in Canada

10 9 8 7 6 5 4 3 2 1

Library of Congress Cataloging-in-Publication Data is available on file.

CONTENTS

INTRODUCTION

Fishing imitations of invertebrates to trout feeding under the surface is usually called nymph fishing, even when the prey you're imitating is a worm or tiny freshwater shrimp. This book covers the easiest and most common flies and techniques used at the turn of the twenty-first century. I purposely excluded "emerger" fishing from this book, because even though it uses a fly that looks like an immature insect, fishing an emerger is really dry-fly fishing—you see the fish rise and take your fly, leaving a visible disturbance on the surface.

Recognizing different kinds of aquatic insects is less important when nymph fishing than when casting a dry fly to rising trout. There's lots of stuff living underwater with the fish all the time, so they are used to seeing and eating a smorgasbord of invertebrates. Insect hatches are fleeting moments, and the trout may see only a single species on the surface at any given time.

Far more important is how you present the fly. It's also important to know something about the life history and behavior of aquatic insects. For instance, 95 percent of mayfly nymphs are feeble swimmers at best, and when drifting in the current are at the mercy of the flow. They never swim across the course of a river, and fishing a nymph "dead-drift," so it appears unattached to a piece of fishing line, will get more strikes in almost every circumstance. Knowing the exceptions, however, can give you an edge.

One very important genus, *Isonychia* (known to fly fishers as the Leadwing Coachman because it was first imitated by a wet fly of that name) is one of the most important summer mayflies in streams like New York's Ausable and Delaware. *Isonychia* swims with the grace of an otter. If you knew your mayflies and turned over a few rocks in the shallows and spied large purplish-brown nymphs darting around like skinny birth-

A single pass through a riffle with a piece of household screen held in the current brought this wide variety of nymphs to light. There is a big stonefly, a mayfly, a cased caddis, two free-living caddis, and three midge larvae in the photo. After reading the next chapter you should be able to identify and imitate them.

INTRODUCTION

day balloons that just sprang leaks, you would immediately attach a Size 12 Zug Bug to your tippet. And instead of the typical method of fishing the nymph with a strike indicator and no movement, you'd strip it across the current like a streamer, drawing vicious strikes from feeding trout.

I don't mean to scare you away with entomology. Identifying aquatic insects may sometimes give you a slight edge, but nearly all mayfly nymphs, midge pupae, free-living caddis larvae, and stonefly nymphs are between Sizes 14 and 20 and are drab-colored. And you can catch almost any trout in the world, except for the real picky ones, if you have Hare's-Ear Nymphs in Sizes 10 through 18, and Pheasant-Tails in Sizes 14 through 22. However, I don't advise limiting your fly selection to this extreme—you'll miss out on the pleasure of experimenting.

CHAPTER 1

NATURALS AND IMITATIONS

MAYFLIES

Entomologists call mayflies the cattle of running-water ecosystems because of their abundance and ability to convert plant fiber into the energy that can be utilized by predators. These insects are found in running water throughout the world. Other than artificial ponds and hatchery tanks, I've never heard of a trout habitat that does not host mayflies. Like many aquatic insects, mayflies live underwater for about 360 days, and hatch and mate at the same time each year, usually from spring through fall depending on the species.

Mayfly nymphs are the cattle of stream ecosystems.

Because a trout stream can support anywhere from a few to dozens of species of mayflies, and each species hatches at different times during the season, the river bottom will always be covered with mayfly nymphs in various stages of development. However, the importance of mayfly nymphs varies more with their availability than their abundance. For example, an examination of a square foot of stream bottom might turn up a hundred large burrowing mayflies of the genus *Ephemera*, commonly known to anglers as the green drake. The same sample might produce only five individuals of the genus *Stenonema*, the fly we call the March brown. The green drakes were buried in the mud, whereas the March browns were crawling around in the shallows where they can easily lose their grip and be swept away in the current and eaten by trout. The fish are used to seeing and eating the March browns, and will eat your fly if it looks and behaves like a March brown. They might ignore a green drake—your imitation or even the real thing.

The tables might turn in a few weeks. All the March browns have hatched and now the green drakes begin to emerge from their mud burrows, drifting for hundreds of feet in the current before hatching. The fish soon recognize green drakes as food and forget those March browns. It's not always so cut-and-dried, though, because a rich trout stream might have a half-dozen mayflies hatching at the same time. Because the fish may be eating all of these mayflies (plus a few species of caddisflies, midges, and stoneflies) in the same afternoon, they won't feed selectively and will probably eat any well-presented nymph.

Mayfly nymphs are often lumped into four broad groups that differ in shape, habitat, and behavior. Knowing into which group a nymph belongs is as far as you need to delve into entomology to be a successful nymph fisher.

Burrowers

These are large mayflies, Sizes 6 through 14, that are nearly always tan or brown. They can be identified by their long, slim bodies, prominent tusks, and feathery gills extending along their abdomens. Their habitat is mud, sand, and silt, and although they are most common in slow water where sediment accumulates on the bottom, they can also be found in faster water where silt collects behind boulders. A casual sampling of the stream bottom won't often turn them up because they are secluded in U-shaped burrows in the substrate. The only way you'll find them is to stir up a silty area of a

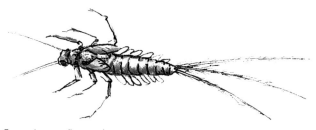

Burrowing mayfly nymph.

NATURALS AND IMITATIONS

river and stand downstream with a seine, capturing the helpless nymphs as they drift in the current.

Burrowers are of tremendous importance close to the times when they hatch, but they are of little importance at other times during the season because they are not easily washed away. However, these nymphs are so meaty and abundant (up to 500 individuals per square foot of bottom have been counted in Midwestern streams) that close to hatch periods they may be the only subsurface food the trout will eat. Burrowers hatch in the East from late May through late July, and emerge in Western rivers from early July through early August. Common names for these nymphs include eastern green drakes, cream variants, Michigan mayflies ("the Hex"), and brown drakes.

If you see large mayflies hatching, or if you hear in a fly shop that one of the above flies is hatching on a river, fish a large tan mayfly imitation close to the bottom with occasional slight twitches. If you spot a few sporadic rises but see none of the big adults disappearing, fish an unweighted nymph dead-drift close to the surface.

Swimmers

These mayflies range from large (Size 10) to very small (Size 22), and all can be recognized by their streamlined shape. They are also called "Minnow Mayflies" because of their shape and behavior. They are among the most widely distributed mayflies in the world, and in spring creeks and tailwaters the tiny ones

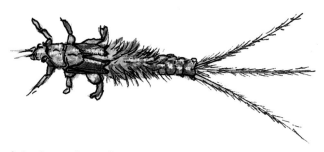

Swimming mayfly nymph.

are often the most important sources of trout food. Unlike the burrowers, they don't stay hidden and are often found prowling along the bottom and in slower currents along the shore. Prior to hatching, they migrate into the shallows in immense numbers, often losing their hold on the bottom and getting swept away. Needless to say, their abundance and availability make them important to both the trout and fly fishermen.

Swimmers can be found in any kind of trout water but are especially abundant in weedy places. The genus *Baetis,* known to fly fishermen as the blue-winged olive, is by far the most common mayfly in spring creeks and tailwaters, but is also abundant in rocky freestone rivers. The *Callibaetis,* or speckled quill, is the most common stillwater mayfly throughout the United States. All swimmers come in mixed shades of dull brown, olive, and gray.

When it comes to behavior, we need to distinguish between the large (Size 14 and bigger) and small (Size 16 and smaller) swimmers. The big ones, known to

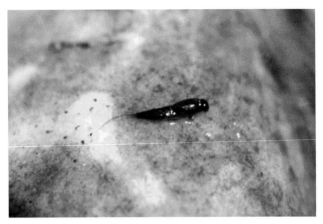

This tiny swimming mayfly nymph is best imitated with a Pheasant-Tail or similar sparse pattern.

fishermen as leadwing coachmen, gray drakes, or speckled quills, are jet-propelled and move with ease along the bottom and in the shallows. They are constantly moving and always available to trout, but the real treat comes up to a week before they hatch and phalanxes of these nymphs migrate into the shallows. Unlike most mayflies, large swimmers hatch by crawling onto midstream rocks and debris along the shore, so the adults are not as important as the nymphs.

The big swimmers hatch from midsummer through early fall, and whether you see some of the big mayflies in the air or not, check along the edges of streams for their cast-off nymph shucks (you can tell them from stonefly shucks by their skinnier and more rounded appearance). You might even spy them swimming along the edge of the river; check carefully for what look like tiny dark fish speeding along the bottom and then darting into debris. Try fishing imitations of these nymphs dead-drift, and if nothing happens, twitch your imitation into the shallows right to your waders. You might be surprised by a huge brown trout trying to grab your fake swimmer before it escapes into thin water.

On the other hand, the little brown and olive ones are feeble swimmers. They crawl and swim in short bursts among the weeds and gravel, but when swept away from the bottom, their meager attempts at swimming make little headway in the current. Imitations of the small swimmers should be fished totally dead-drift; any twitch with rod tip or line hand will be far too overt and unnatural. Flies suspended from a strike indicator in fast currents probably furnish an accept-

A slim imitation with sparse legs imitates the bigger swimmers.

able imitation of this swimming movement. Tiny swimmers hatch throughout the season, from March through November, and on any given day you will probably find at least a few individuals hatching. On cold, rainy days, hatches of these guys are heavy, and small, slim nymphs will be deadly all day long even if you never see a trout rising to adult mayflies.

The best flies to imitate the swimmers are slim patterns with no legs or very sparse hackle. Artificial nymphs tied with feather fibers or feather quills, like the Pheasant-Tail or Zug Bug, are more effective than fuzzier patterns tied with fur.

Crawlers

Crawlers are similar in shape to the swimmers, but are more oval in shape and even the largest species cannot swim. In freestone rivers, they are the most important and abundant mayflies, and such beloved hatches as hendricksons, pale evening duns, pale-morning duns, and Western green drakes emerge from crawling nymphs. They are most often found in fast-moving rivers with lots of gravel. Here they crawl across the bottom, especially on the underside of rocks, and when grabbed by the current they alternate between wiggling their bodies and drifting stiffly extended, like an Olympic diver poised in midair.

Besides easy availability to trout, crawlers can be astoundingly abundant. Samples taken in fertile rivers may turn up hundreds of nymphs in a square foot of stream bottom. Their body shape is typically half-

Crawlers, found in most riffles, can be astoundingly abundant.

round, with feeble legs and tails. Colors are nearly always shades of tan or brown with olive tints, and they range from Sizes 12 to 22. Like most mayflies, crawlers become more active a few days before hatching, and about an hour prior to emerging they begin drifting helplessly in the current and rising toward the surface. At this time, nymphs can be found from the bottom of a river to just under the surface, and trout feed more regularly, actively chasing the nymphs. If you know what time the mayflies will hatch, you can have over an hour of very exciting nymph fishing. This is not as hard to figure out as it sounds.

Typical crawler shape.

This crawler imitation sports a flashy wing case to catch a trout's attention.

For instance, hendrickson mayflies hatch promptly at 3 P.M. in early May. From experience, I know I can fish a hendrickson nymph imitation (a plain Gold-Ribbed Hare's-Ear works just fine) all morning long and pick up a fish or two in three hours of fishing. From 2 P.M. to 3 P.M. however, it's like someone flipped a switch, and the same fly, fished the same way, can produce three times as many trout as the entire morning. Similarly, the smaller pale evening duns hatch just before dark in early June, and the same thing happens from 7 P.M. to 8 P.M.

Flies used to imitate these mayfly nymphs should be moderately plump, between the skinny shape of the swimmers and the bulky profile of the flattened crawlers. Legs and tails should not be too heavy to imitate the sparse appendages of the naturals.

Flattened Crawlers

Flattened crawlers are easily distinguished from all other mayfly nymphs by their flattened heads with eyes on top, robust legs, and thick tails. In most species, the abdominal gills are flat and wide, and act like tiny suction cups, keeping the nymphs firmly attached to the undersides of rocks. These are fast-water mayflies. They thrive in water that rushes so fast you would not think any insect could live there. These mayflies are usually found in colors from tan to rust to dark brown, and won't be found unless there is an abundance of flat rocks in a river.

Flattened crawlers are usually quite large, from Size 10 to 16, and they are the mayflies most often ob-

Flattened crawlers are perfectly adapted for living under flat rocks in fast water.

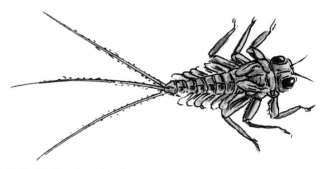

Typical flattened crawler shape.

served when you turn over flat rocks in the streambed. Because they adhere so tightly to the underside of rocks, they're not as readily available to trout—as long as they aren't hatching. A few days before they hatch, however, these nymphs always migrate to the shallows, exposing themselves to the current and to eager trout. Because they typically hatch all day long, unlike the crawlers, you can have superb nymph fishing all day while a hatch of these flies is in progress.

Despite their robust appearance, flattened crawlers can't swim at all, so nymphs fished dead-drift in deep, fast runs and in rocky shallows work best. Flies used to imitate them should be fat, wide, and fuzzy, with thick tails and lots of hackle. Common names of mayfly hatches of flattened crawlers include the Western and Eastern March brown, quill Gordon, light Cahill, gray fox, and Western red quill. These insects are some of the first large mayflies of the season to

The Hare's-Ear Nymph's fuzziness imitates the flattened shape, robust legs, and feathery gills of a flattened crawler.

hatch, and are active from March through June west of the Mississippi, and from April through early July in the East.

CADDISFLIES

Caddisflies rival mayflies as underwater trout food, and in some kinds of streams they are more abundant than mayflies and extremely important to trout. The larvae are far more diverse in shape and size than mayflies, and take many different forms. The most typical and easily recognized form is the type that builds a case from pebbles, sticks, shells, or leaf litter. These crawl across the bottom, clumsily dragging a cylindrical case, but the case is a benefit rather than a liability because without its ballast the larvae would be swept away in the current. Some larvae make half-round or purse-shaped cases that cling tightly to rocks.

Four types of caddis larvae. The top two species are free-living, while the bottom two build cases.

Other small caddisflies build tubes in sand or mud on the bottom. Net-spinners construct spiderlike webs in crevices between rocks and strain their food from the flow. And finally, there are free-living, predatory forms that crawl along the bottom under rocks, living without cases except during pupation.

Regardless of their protection, caddis larvae are distinguished by their soft, grub-like abdomen, hard, shiny thorax with a pair of single-clawed feet on each segment, and small head without visible antennae. There is a pair of hooks at the end of the abdomen and no wing case on the thorax.

Unlike mayflies, which hatch directly from larvae into adults, caddisflies have true metamorphosis, which

This artificial imitates a caddis larva stretching outside of its case.

means there is an aquatic pupa as well as a larva stage. The larvae live underwater for just about twelve months. A week or two before emerging, the larvae cease feeding and moving. Even the free-living forms build stone cases, and those already living in cases retreat to one end of the case and cement it firmly to a rock or log. For this short time caddisflies are beyond the reach of trout, but once pupation is complete, they leave their cases and drift in the current for a few minutes to a few hours. At first they drift close to the bottom, but then their exoskeletons fill with gases which quickly buoy the pupae to the surface. Trout feed heavily on drifting pupae and might ignore any other food. Some pupae drift helplessly but others are strong swimmers and oar themselves across the current, so it pays to put your nose close to the water to see how the naturals are behaving. If the pupae merely drift in the current, a dead-drift presentation is best; if you see them twitching through the water, a wet-fly swing or a dead drift alternated with subtle twitches will draw more strikes.

There is no way to tell when trout are feeding on caddis larvae unless you see a trout grubbing on the bottom, turning over rocks. You read about this bottom-grubbing in the outdoor press, but in my experience it's rare, and most caddis larvae get eaten when they are swept away by the current. This is not as uncommon as you might suspect because as the case-makers grow they must periodically shed their cases. At this stage the larva is a helpless grub and often finds itself drifting in the current. Now a trout can merely pluck the caddis larva from the drift. Even if you can see a trout doing this, you really don't know if it's eating a mayfly, stonefly, midge, or caddisfly.

Trout feeding on pupae often show distinctive behavior that you can observe at the surface. Although pupae are available to trout for only a tiny fraction of their life cycles, they are far more vulnerable than larvae. Because the pupae of some species swim against the current, and other species rise quickly to the surface, trout follow them aggressively, taking the insects well under the surface and betraying their activity with splashy bulges in the water. The next time you're sitting in the bathtub, cup your hand and pretend to grab something below the surface with a quick motion. You'll see a hump in the water that often forms a

Typical caddis pupa shape and drab color.

splash, even though your hand never comes near the surface. The key to recognizing this feeding behavior is to look for a smooth bulging rise with an absence of bubbles. A trout rising to an adult insect inhales air as it sucks in its prey; the air is expelled right after the rise, creating bubbles. Rises to mayflies just under the surface can look the same, but caddisfly bulges are usually louder and more violent.

Because caddisfly adults look similar (mostly drab and mothlike) and the larvae are varied and tough to identify, caddisflies don't have as many common names as mayflies and fishermen tend to lump them together and use more generic imitations. They range in size from the giant Size 8 October caddis, which makes its case from twigs and crawls across the bottom, to the dinky and irritating Size 22 microcaddis (irritating because when they are hatching you often can't tell what the trout are eating, and once you figure it out, they're still tough to fool). Most species of caddisflies fit conveniently into the Size 14 to 18 range. Free-living larvae are mostly drab and well camou-

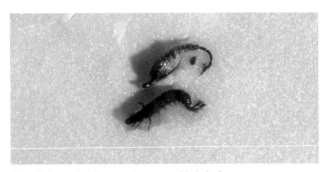

A free-living caddis larva and a reasonable imitation.

flaged in shades of tan, brown, and olive. Larvae that live inside cases are often pale, from almost pure white to light tan, and when they shed their cases trout spot them easily. Some of the net-spinning larvae are bright green. Pupae are invariably drab, in shades of gray, brown, tan, and olive.

Unlike the more widely studied mayflies, imitations of specific species of caddisflies are rare. Instead, we try to cover a wide variety of larvae and pupae sizes and colors with generic imitations. For instance, in my fly boxes I always have imitations of green free-living and net-spinning larvae made of green fur with black or brown fur heads, some cased imitations like a rough Hare's-Ear Nymph, and some white or light tan nymphs that represent the pale saddle or purse-shaped larvae that have outgrown their cases. Most of my pupae imitations are brown or olive, and because trout see drifting pupae in concentrated numbers and can feed on

Caddis pupa imitation.

them more selectively, I carry a wider variety. Flies with brass tungsten beads at their heads imitate pupae drifting close to the bottom. The bead adds weight to the fly and also imitates the sparkle of gas bubbles inside the insect. Because tungsten is heavier than brass, I use these for fast, deep water; I use the flies with brass heads for shallower, slower currents. For pupae drifting in mid-water and close to the surface, I like a pupa with a shuck of Antron yarn to mimic the translucence of the air bubble surrounding the emerging insect.

STONEFLIES

Stoneflies are most common in cold, clear, highly oxygenated water. In fact, they are often used as indicator species—their sudden absence can signal a problem with water quality because they are intolerant of warm,

Stonefly nymphs are flattened like some mayflies, but the gills are under the thorax instead of along the abdomen.

silty, or polluted water. Stoneflies look a lot like flattened mayfly nymphs, but you can tell them apart because stoneflies have large, feathery gills under the thorax and two sets of wing pads instead of the single pair you see on mayfly nymphs. Like mayflies, they have incomplete metamorphosis, without a pupal stage, and the flattened nymphs hatch directly into adults.

The faster the water, the more trout depend on stoneflies in their diets. In a tumbling, high-altitude river with a steep slope, stoneflies might represent a third of a trout population's diet. Once the same river settles down to placid flows in the valley, stoneflies are not as dominant and are of less importance to the trout. In spring creeks and lakes, stoneflies are rare because the slow currents do not deliver enough oxygen.

Stoneflies don't usually hatch like mayflies, drifting in the current before breaking the surface and emerg-

Stonefly shucks along the riverbank give you a clue on what imitation to use.

ing as adults. When water temperatures and time of year are suitable for hatching, the nymphs of a species will migrate into the shallows or to the edges of large midstream rocks. The nymphs then crawl out of the water and split their exoskeletons on land, and the adults crawl away until their wings are dry. You'll often find the shed skins of stonefly nymphs on rocks along the riverbank, and sometimes two or three feet up the trunks of trees beside the water.

Four different types of stonefly imitations.

Stoneflies range from the giant Size 4 or 6 salmonfly of the West, to as small as Size 18. Some may go through several life cycles per season, and a few of the big ones live as nymphs for two or three years before hatching. Most stonefly nymphs have twelve-month life cycles like mayflies and caddisflies. All stoneflies are relatively flat in shape, but the smaller ones are proportionally longer and skinnier than the big ones. Most are colored shades of black, brown, or tan, with tints of yellow, olive, and even orange.

Because of their flattened shape and hatching behavior, you'd think stonefly nymphs would not often be available to drift-feeding trout. However, stonefly nymphs do a substantial amount of active crawling and foraging on the bottom, and they are present in the drift with other kinds of insects. Prior to hatching, they're extremely active when migrating to the shallows and may become more important than any other kind of insect. Unlike mayflies and caddisflies, stoneflies hatch year-round; the small black insect commonly known as the snowfly is a stonefly that hatches in the dead of winter and spends much of its time crawling around on snow banks.

Stoneflies cannot swim, although they do wiggle and undulate their bodies when drifting in the current. Because they drift helplessly and don't rise toward the surface to hatch, flies used to imitate them should be either tied with lots of weight (or fished with weight on the leader), and dead-drift techniques that get the

Scale of most common sizes in stonefly nymphs. The big brown one is a Size 6, about 1½ inches long. The tiny amber one is about ¼ inch long, about a Size 18.

fly close to the bottom are best. Although you have hundreds of imitations of stonefly nymphs from which to choose, your selection doesn't need to be very extensive. The most common stonefly throughout the world is called the golden stone, and a tan or yellowish nymph in Sizes 8 to 12 will imitate them. For early spring fishing, a Size 14 Dark Brown Stonefly and a Size 16 or 18 Black Stonefly will match the types that emerge in the early season before mayflies and caddisflies get active. If you fish in the Rocky Mountains or in mountain streams of the West Coast, it's critical to have some very large dark stoneflies to imitate the salmonfly or giant stonefly. These insects hatch from mid-June to August, but since they may live two or three years as nymphs, there are always big ones crawling along the bottom of fast, rocky streams.

Paying attention to water types when fishing mayfly and caddisfly imitations is not always important, because these insects live in all water types. When hatching, they can drift from fast riffles into the tail of a pool hundreds of yards away. Stonefly nymphs, however, should be fished only in fast water with some rocks at least as wide as dinner plates. Stonefly larvae don't exist anywhere else, and they crawl into the shallows when hatching, seldom drifting into slow pools below fast water.

MIDGES

Midges are one of the most important but ignored sources of aquatic trout food. In slow, weedy, or silty

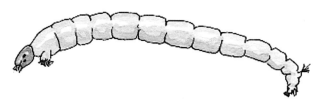

Midge larva. They come in a wide variety of colors, from blood red to bright green to white.

water, the bottom of a river may harbor thousands of midge larvae per square foot. Midges are particularly important in stillwaters; in many lakes they are the primary source of trout food. Similarly, in tailwater rivers below dams, midges find perfect habitat as nutrient-rich lake water, controlled by dam releases to prevent flooding and scouring of the bottom, passes over a stream bed that is usually full of aquatic vegetation and silt. Midges become the dominant invertebrates as currents slow, but they can be found anywhere; a small patch of silt behind a rock or along the shore can harbor hundreds of midge larvae.

Midges are not always tiny, and both larvae and adults can be as large as a Size 14 hook. But the typical stream-dwelling midge is between a Size 18 and 24. The bad news is that some can be even smaller than a Size 32 hook—too small to imitate. The good news is that trout seldom feed selectively on the very tiny ones. In weedy tailwaters like Colorado's South Platte and Frying Pan, the Bighorn in Montana, the San Juan in New Mexico, and Arkansas's White River,

Assorted midge larvae and pupae imitations. Trout can be quite selective about size and color, despite the natural's tiny size.

midges are the primary source of trout food, especially close to the dams. You can watch huge browns and rainbows, swaying in the current, constantly sliding back and forth, eating seemingly invisible food. Juicy mayflies drift over them and the fish don't even wiggle a fin. Toss a meaty grasshopper above them and they'll ignore it.

How do you know when trout are eating midges under the surface? A good clue is their complete disregard for any visible food. Weeds on the bottom or along the edges of a river are another clue. Pick up a handful of weeds, and if the vegetation is full of tiny red or green wiggling worms, you have a pretty good idea of the food source. Finally, one of the best ways of knowing when to fish midges is to check books, fly-shop counters, and guide recommendations. If you see flies like the Desert Storm or Disco Midge in Size 22 recommended for a certain river, you know midge-eating trout are present. No one likes to tie these tiny bugs on a 7X tippet unless he has to!

Because trout eat so many midges in the course of a day, they get very selective as to the size of the fly. Prior to a trip to the San Juan in the middle of winter, I tied several dozen midge larvae in Sizes 20 and 22, which is usually as small as I need to go in familiar rivers in the West. On a whim, I called Johnny Gomez, a superb guide on the San Juan, and he said, "We're

On rich tailwaters like the San Juan, the right midge nymph is important to success.

Midge pupae drift in the current all day long.

fishing mainly Size 24 Desert Storms lately." I'm glad I tied up another dozen in Size 24, because the day I floated with Johnny, the fish showed a very clear preference for the Size 24s—even over a Size 22. To you and me, these sizes look the same (both too damn tiny!), but there is a real difference to the fish.

Why are these little specks, about the size of a capital letter in this book, so popular with the trout? First, their abundance is hard to ignore. Trout key into food they know is safe and edible, and where a trout might see a dozen mayfly nymphs pass by in an hour, it could see hundreds of midges. Second, midges may be a favorite trout food because of their taste. Studies comparing an insect's abundance in the drift to the percentage in a trout's stomach indicate they may favor midges. Third, unlike mayflies and caddisflies, which drift in distinct periods just after dark and before sunrise, midges drift all day long—when they are easiest for drift-feeding trout to spot them. And lastly, the bigger the fly, the better trout can spot its fraud and the more suspicious they are. Small flies appear to be safer to trout in heavily fished waters.

Midges, like caddisflies, have complete metamorphosis with a pupal stage. Although some larvae burrow in the muck, others are free-living and crawl among aquatic vegetation from which they are frequently dislodged. Pupae drift for a long time in the current prior to hatching, but some rise quickly to the surface. Here they are eaten by trout with visible surface rises, something we won't cover in this book. However, the pupae of many drift close to the bottom and in mid-water for hours on end, and are eaten by trout with no sign of surface feeding.

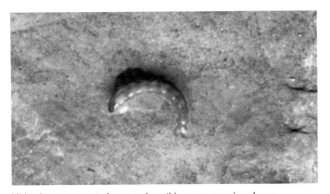

Midge larvae are not always red, as this cream species shows.

NATURALS AND IMITATIONS

Midge larvae are tiny wormlike creatures with one pair of tiny legs called prolegs at the thorax and another pair at the far end. They have no visible tails or antennae. The head is tiny and black; the segmented body can be brown, green, purple, cream, or bright red. I find the red ones (called bloodworms) to be the most common in trout streams, with the green ones coming in second. Interestingly, the red ones actually contain hemoglobin, which helps transport oxygen in their bodies, allowing them to live in water with very low oxygen levels. But midge larvae are just as abundant in highly oxygenated trout streams. Midge larvae imitations are as simple as flies get—red or green thread or floss wrapped on a hook with a black thread head.

Midge pupae look similar to caddis pupae but are slimmer and more segmented, especially in the abdomen. There are feathery gills at the head, and the thorax is quite thick in relation to the abdomen, with a thick lump under the thorax that contains the emerging legs and wings. They are always drab in color, usually shades of brown, tan, or olive with black segmentation. Midge pupae develop a gas bubble under the exoskeleton to help buoy them to the surface and perhaps assist with emerging. Pupae imitations are usually simple, with quill or thread bodies and fur thoraxes. Fancier versions are available, however, with feathery gills imitated by marabou, wing cases of epoxied floss, and gas bubbles under the body imitated by wraps of narrow holographic tinsel or a tiny glass bead at the head.

I love fishing midge nymphs. Most people hate the thought of fishing a Size 24 nymph close to the bottom

Big trout eat small midge nymphs.

with lead in water too deep to spot trout, but it is a fascinating and productive way to catch trout all year long. Fishing midge nymphs may be the only way to catch trout on a fly from November through March because midges are active all winter and may be the only aquatic insects drifting in the current during daylight hours. And in rivers where midges are abundant, trout will eat larvae and pupae even at the height of mayfly and caddisfly hatches. Knowing this, and realizing that trout will be far less suspicious of your midge pupa than your Size 12 Green Drake Nymph, can be a powerful secret and allow you to catch trout when everyone else has given up hope.

When drifting, midge larvae alternate between tiny wiggles and a stiff, motionless profile. Don't try to imitate the squirming—no twitches can imitate this motion. Just fish midge larvae dead-drift with absolutely no drag or added action. You must get your imitation as close to the trout as possible because although a fish might eat over 500 midge larvae an hour, it won't move more than a few inches for each one. Studies have shown that the larger the prey, the farther a trout will move for it. You might get a trout to move three feet for a streamer, or a foot for a big stonefly nymph, but you'll be lucky if one moves six inches to take your midge nymph.

You can try a slight upward movement with a midge pupa imitation to mimic its rise to the surface, but most times you'll have more success fishing the pupa as close to the current speed and as close to the bottom as possible. This is not so bad when you can see trout feeding in shallow water and watch their reactions to the fly (which can be heart-thumping fun). If you have to fish deeper water and can't watch the fish, you'll still need to maintain that dead drift, which gets much tougher as the water gets deeper because surface currents try to pull your fly off the bottom. It's not as much fun, but in the dead of winter it's a sweet alternative to bowling.

OTHER AQUATIC INSECTS

Craneflies

Craneflies, like midges, are true flies and relatives of mosquitoes, black flies, horseflies, and other beloved stream companions. The adults are the familiar flying "daddy long legs" that you see on your screens in summer. The larvae are featureless grubs and look as much like an adult cranefly as a caterpillar does a butterfly. Only some cranefly larvae are aquatic, and even those that live in trout streams live in mud and moss along the banks, not in the river itself. The larvae are anywhere from a half-inch to three inches long, but most are right around an inch and come in shades of brown or tan.

These grubs are not often seen by trout, but when a flood raises the flow and rushes into the ground at the margin of a river, cranefly larvae can get swept into the river in great numbers. When this happens, trout feed heavily on them, just as they do earthworms after a rain. One difference between cranefly larvae and earthworms is that cranefly larvae swim quite well, in an undulating manner, extending and contracting their fleshy bodies.

Cranefly larvae imitations are fished in Western rivers where the insect population has been studied by anglers—the South Platte in Colorado, and the Madison in Montana in particular. Because there is no way a fisherman observing from above can tell if and when fish are eating cranefly larvae, I suspect they are important in more rivers than we suppose all over the country. The next time you're faced with rising water, try something that looks like a cranefly larva.

You'll need two patterns to imitate cranefly larvae. One is a fat, cylindrical nymph to mimic a motionless adult tumbling in the drift; a Size 10 Hare's-Ear Nymph or similar large brownish fly, fished dead-drift,

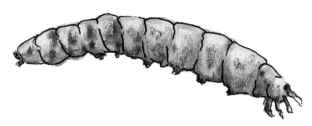

Cranefly larvae look sedentary but are fast swimmers.

will suffice. Another pattern that you should have is a Size 8, skinny brown leech to imitate a swimming larva. This one should be fished by alternating dead drift with foot-long strips.

Damselflies and Dragonflies

Damsels and dragons are more commonly seen in lakes than moving water, but damselflies may be abundant in the back eddies of slow-moving rivers, spring creeks, and beaver ponds. Both insects have incomplete metamorphosis so the adults hatch directly from the nymph without a pupa stage. Damselfly and dragonfly nymphs are probably easy for most people to identify, but they can be distinguished from other aquatic invertebrates by their bug-like eyes that are wider than their thoraxes, and gills at the end of their abdomens. Damselflies are slim and have three feather-like tail gills; dragonflies are fat and wide, and have no visible gills. If you turn them over, both larvae have huge, wide lower jaws that shoot out to capture prey.

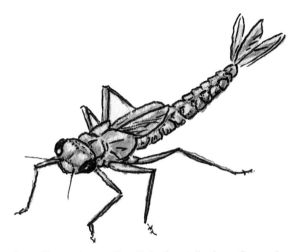

Damselfly nymphs are slim with feathery tails; dragonfly nymphs are fat and wide.

Both insects prowl aquatic vegetation looking for prey, and they'll eat anything from midge larvae to small fish. They crawl and swim, and some species make short bursts by expelling water through the end of their abdomens. Damselflies are the more common of the two and rival midges as the most important stillwater insect. You never find a serious stillwater angler without a box full of damselfly nymphs, but you'd have to track down a real diehard to find a box loaded with dragonfly nymphs. Imitations of both bugs should be in shades of olive (most common), tan, and brown. You might be able to get away with a basic brown/olive nymph like a Prince or Zug Bug for a damsel imitation, but stillwater trout get such a good look at your fly that it's wise to carry several different sizes and patterns of damselfly nymphs if you fish in lakes.

Imitations of both flies should be fished either slow and steady, drawing the fly through the water with long pulls on the line, or with short, sharp strips alternated with pauses to let the fly sink. Although the naturals can swim rapidly, I've found it easier to fool trout with the slow retrieve. Because these insects are active during daylight hours, flies can be fished all day long with success.

Aquatic Bugs

Most aquatic bugs, like the giant water bug and water scorpion, secrete noxious chemicals that keep them from being eaten by fish and other predators. The familiar water boatman that you see sculling just below the surface of lakes and slow streams is an exception, and is a preferred trout food. Fish often move three or four feet to capture one. The Corixa Bug (a common name derived from its family name, Corixidae) is a common stillwater nymph in England, but fishing these imitations is uncommon in the United States. One exception is the upper Colorado River region, where Marty Cecil and his superb guides at Elktrout Lodge rely heavily on backswimmer imitations for adrenaline-pumping action.

Backswimmers are active fliers and disperse from one pond to another by launching themselves into the air, flying to the next pond, dive-bombing the surface, and then calmly swimming as if they'd been present

Backswimmers offer exciting fishing in ponds.

all along. Although trout will eat backswimmers when-
ever they find them, the fish are really on the lookout
for the splat of a new arrival to their pond. Marty's
technique is to make a powerful cast with a nymph so
it makes a hard splash when entering the water. Then
he strips the fly quickly, taunting an interested trout
into eating the fly. Sometimes trout pursue the fly ten
or fifteen feet, leaving wakes like incoming torpedoes.
This is easy and exciting fishing, compounded by the
backswimmers' inclination to do this in the middle of
bright afternoons, when few other insects are active.

There are a few commercial backswimmer imitations on the market, especially if you have access to
flies from England. In a pinch, a large scud or Bead-
Head Caddis nymph in Sizes 12 or 14 will work.

Beetles, Ants, and Grasshoppers

There are two situations where flies we commonly
think of as terrestrials can be fished like nymphs. First,
some species of beetles are aquatic and spend their en-

tire life cycles, from larva to pupa to adult, beneath the surface. Second, all kinds of terrestrial insects fall into the water, and not all of them float for long. We usually think of terrestrial patterns as dry flies—hoppers, beetles, and crickets. We see the insects lying helpless on the surface, we see trout rise to them, and we see our flies inhaled by nice fish. But many of these hapless insects tumble into the water and sink, and trout probably eat just as many of them under the water. To catch these trout, try fishing terrestrial imitations as nymphs.

Aquatic water-beetle larvae look like free-living caddis larvae, the distinguishing features being small to large spines protruding from each abdominal section and a lack of wing pads on the thorax. I don't think you need to know the difference; I doubt if trout can tell them apart, and the trout will eat caddis larvae imitations if they are eating beetle larvae. Adult aquatic beetles look just like their terrestrial relatives: shiny, round, and usually dark brown or black. You can imitate these with a regular floating beetle imitation; pinch a small amount of weight on your leader a foot or so above the fly to keep it down, and fish it upstream dead-drift as you would any other nymph.

To imitate terrestrial insects that have fallen into the water and drowned, fish your flies in the same manner with a split shot or a small lump of soft weight a foot above the fly. Sinking ants are available commercially; my fishing buddy Pat Neuner uses a sinking ant fly as often as he does any other nymph and takes fish when they won't eat standard mayfly and caddisfly imitations. Many anglers let their floating grasshopper imitations sink halfway through the drift and watch for the swirl of a trout taking the fly just under the surface.

Sunken terrestrial fishing is an ace-in-the-hole technique that often fools trout that won't respond to any other technique. I first saw grasshopper imitations fished wet on purpose, with weight on the leader and a strike indicator, by Steve Kenerk on Wyoming's Popo Agie River. He found that trout reluctant to come to the surface for a dry grasshopper were far less suspicious of the sunken fly, and he could catch fish in pools where they would never come to the surface. I watched him pull several trout from a pool after I had fished through the water with a dry grasshopper and a succession of mayfly and stonefly nymphs. He put a dry 'hopper imitation on his leader, enough split shot to get the fly almost to the bottom, and a big yarn indicator to suspend the fly and tell when a trout had taken his offering. This same rig can be used with dry beetle, ant, and even tiny leafhopper imitations.

CRUSTACEANS

Crustaceans are important trout foods because they are always available and active. They don't hatch and leave the water like aquatic insects, so there is no time of year when the water is barren of them. Additionally, aquatic insects go through a period of diapause or hibernation when they can't be seen, and even sampling of the stream bottom fails to turn them up. This typically happens during the winter, although some forms enter diapause during the summer. Crustacean imitations are especially important during the winter and early spring when insects may be still buried in the mud. Crustaceans, especially scuds and sow bugs, are most common in alkaline waters because they need the dissolved calcium to build their exoskeletons. Alkaline waters are usually identified by the heavy weed growth seen in spring-fed streams and tailwaters. Crustaceans are most active in low light levels, so imitations of them are best used in early morning and late evening.

Crayfish

Trout enthusiastically eat crayfish of all sizes, from tiny inch-long juveniles to four-inch adults. Large trout are especially fond of them, and where crayfish

Big trout will go out of their way to capture small crayfish.

are common they may be as important as baitfish to the trophy trout. Large crayfish are usually pursued when disturbed by predators and are better imitated with a streamer like a Woolly Bugger and an active retrieve. The tiny ones, however, aren't strong swimmers, and when they get swept into the current they drift just like a big stonefly or mayfly nymph. You can buy or tie imitations of small crayfish, but I've found that a brown stonefly or a large mayfly nymph imitation like a March Brown will fool trout when I suspect they are eating tiny crayfish. In waters with dense crayfish populations, fish your nymph at first light with a dead-drift presentation.

Sow Bugs

Sow bugs are related to the common "pill bugs" you see in your garden and look just like them. You will find these crustaceans only in slow-moving waters with aquatic weeds, like spring creeks, rich tailwaters, or ponds. They are mostly gray or olive, flattened dorsally, and have lots of legs sticking out on the sides. Sow bugs cannot swim but get knocked off their weedy perches. I have seen trout in Pennsylvania's Letort Spring Run rush into a clump of weeds, thrash the weeds with their jaws, then slide back and inhale the dislodged sow bugs. This behavior is apparently pretty common in shallow water in the early morning or on dark, rainy days when sow bugs are active.

The most common way to fish sow-bug imitations is to quietly stalk the banks of a weedy trout stream in

Look for trout eating sow bugs in clumps of weed in shallow water.

early morning, looking for fish lying in shallow water. Carefully cast a sow-bug nymph a few feet above the trout so it sinks to its level. You usually leave weight and strike indicators off your leader to prevent spooking the fish with the splash. Getting the proper lead on your cast without alarming the fish is a challenge, but is one of the most satisfying ways of taking a trout on a nymph.

Scuds

Scuds are similar to sow bugs, but are instead laterally compressed. They live in the same kinds of weedy streams and are usually more abundant and more active than sow bugs. Also unlike sow bugs, scuds can swim and are commonly found darting between weed beds where they are speared by predatory trout. Most of the famous tailwater rivers in the United States, such as the Bighorn, San Juan, Colorado, and White, have large populations of scuds. These rivers grow fat,

A simple but flashy scud imitation.

healthy trout because scuds are so high in calories. Most common sizes are between a No. 10 and 18 hook, and colors are shades of olive, gray, and tan. Some scud imitations are pink or orange, imitating dead scuds drifting in the current. Fish in certain rivers seem to prefer the bright ones, perhaps because they are easier to spot.

Scuds curl into a crescent shape when disturbed or at rest, and extend in a straight line when swimming. You'll hear arguments in fly shops and along the river-bank as to which form should be imitated, so just carry both. Trout eat moving scuds as eagerly as they eat swimming ones. I have found that the smaller your im-itation, the more readily trout will eat it, perhaps be-cause they are less wary of a small fly.

Scuds are flattened laterally and are more active than sow bugs.

A Flashback Scud imitation fooled this nice rainbow for veteran Montana guide Dave Kumlein. Note the rich, weedy environment.

Scud imitations can be cast to visibly feeding trout in shallow water or to unseen fish in fast or deep water. Strike indicators and weight are usually left off the leader when sight-casting to keep from spooking the trout. In fast riffles or in deep water, you'll need some weight to get the fly down and a strike indicator so you can see when the fish take the fly. Dead drift is usually the best presentation, but because scuds do swim, an occasional twitch may help interest reluctant fish.

AQUATIC WORMS

Aquatic worms look just like the earthworms you find crawling on the sidewalk after a rain but are only

An aquatic worm from New Mexico's San Juan River, alongside the famous San Juan Worm imitation.

about an inch in length when not extended. They live in mud and silt in the shallows and are especially common in tailwaters. These creatures don't actively swim but get swept into the current by floods and wading anglers. Worm flies are deadly when floods or tailwater releases wash into the shallows and dislodge the real worms. In many rivers, worms are so abundant that trout will gorge on them to the exclusion of other foods.

Worm-eating trout are most often spotted at the edges of shallow riffles. When wading in very rich tailwaters such as the San Juan or South Platte, you will often develop a cadre of trout that will follow you around like a litter of puppies. They're picking up worms and midge larvae disturbed by your wading. A technique called "shuffling" developed where the bottom is purposely disturbed and a fly is dangled downstream in the stirred-up plume of food. This is not only tacky, it's actually illegal on many rivers. Even with careful wading, though, you can't help but develop a fan club in some riffles, and I have seen fishermen go through amazing contortions, casting the fly straight up in the air and slightly upstream, in an attempt to drift it right at their feet.

BASIC NYMPH SELECTIONS

The Essential Dozen

PATTERN	BEST WATER TYPES TO USE	SIZES	IMITATES
Hare's Ear (Bead-Head, Tunghead, and regular versions depending on water depth)	• Riffles • Runs • Pocket water • Pools	8–18	• Burrowing mayfly nymphs • Crawling mayfly nymphs • Flattened crawling mayfly nymphs • Free-living and cased caddis larve • Caddis pupae • Larger stonefly nymphs • Sow bugs
Pheasant Tail (Bead-Head, Tunghead, and regular versions depending on water depth)	• Slow pools • Shallow riffles • Spring creeks • Tailwaters • Ponds	14–20	• Swimming mayfly nymphs • Midge larvae • Midge pupae • Crawling mayfly nymphs • Small stonefly nymphs

Golden Stonefly	• Faster water with large rocks	8–12	• Larger, light-colored stonefly nymphs
Bead-Head Caddis Pupa (olive, brown, and cream)	• Riffles • Runs • Pocket water • Pools	12–18	• Caddis pupae (deep drifting) • Scuds • Water boatman
LaFontaine Sparkle Pupa	• Riffles • Runs • Pocket water • Pools	12–18	• Caddis pupae (emerging)
Prince (Bead-Head, Tunghead, and regular versions depending on water depth)	• Riffles • Runs • Pocket water • Pools	10–16	• Stoneflies • Crawling mayflies 

Fly	Water	Size	Imitates
Zug Bug (Bead-Head, Tunghead, and regular versions depending on water depth)	• Riffles • Runs • Pocket water • Pools	10–16	• Swimming mayflies • Crawling mayflies • Damselflies
Bead-Body Scud (olive, orange, pink)	• Spring creeks • Tailwaters • Ponds	12–16	• Scuds
Bead-Head Stonefly (black and brown versions)	• Faster water with large rocks	6–10	• Large stoneflies • Small crayfish (brown color) • Hellgrammites (black version)
Brassie	• Pools • Tailwaters • Spring creeks	16–20	• Midge larvae • Midge pupae

Vernille San Juan Worm	• Tailwaters	8–12	• Aquatic worms
(red and tan versions)			

Halfback	• Riffles	8–14	• Stoneflies
	• Runs		• Small crayfish
	• Pocket water		• Flattened crawling mayflies

CHAPTER 2

NYMPH FISHING TACKLE

There is really no special tackle needed for nymph fishing. The same outfit you choose for dry flies or streamers will be just fine for nymph fishing. In fact, although I enjoy nymph fishing as much as casting dries to rising fish, all of the nymph rigs I use, from rod to line to leader, can be modified to fish dry flies in less than 30 seconds.

RODS AND REELS

There are experts who will tell you that a rod at least 9 feet long is essential for proper nymphing. I guess they've never seen Ed Schenk, the wizard of the Letort, nymph for big sow-bug-eating brown trout with his 6½-foot 4-weight rod, or guide and TV personality Rick Wollum fool one South Platte rainbow after another with his 7-foot, 9-inch 2-weight. It depends on the water type you're fishing. In big rivers, or those with tricky, contrary currents, you might need a big rod to keep as much fly line off the water as possible, especially when fishing up-and-across stream or directly across stream. However, if you're sneaking up on big trout from directly behind, or fishing straight upstream in tiny mountain brooks, a long rod isn't needed and may even be a hindrance. So pick the length by water type.

When fishing big water or big nymphs from a boat, a longer, heavier rod is a good idea.

Your rod's line size should match the kind of fishing you expect to do. A 6-weight rod is best for very large nymphs, heavy water, and the giant indicators they sometimes use in the Rockies. Fishing Size 4 Salmonfly Nymphs from a drift boat would be typical of a situation where you would want a 6-weight rod. On the other hand, if all your nymph fishing is in a tailwater or spring creek where a Size 16 nymph is a giant and the trout are very spooky, you might never want a rod bigger than a 3-weight. Use a 4-weight in rivers where most of the flies will be small, where trout might be spooky, and most of the indicators you use will be small and not too air resistant. The 5-weight is really today's all-around line size, and a 5-

weight rod can run the gamut. It will be pushing a bit too hard with a big stonefly and No. 5 split shot, and it might spook some fish taking Size 24 midges in quiet water—but you can almost always make a 5-weight rod do the trick.

Use any reel you find suitable for the rod. If someone tells you one reel is better for nymph fishing than another, count your fingers before walking away.

LINES

You could fish with nymphs all your life and never use anything other than a floating line. I can't remember the last time I used a sinking or sink-tip line when nymphing in running water (although I often use them for nymphs in lakes and for streamers in big rivers). The only time you may find a need for a sinking-tip line would be at the head of a huge pool with a whirlpool on the side and you know you have to get down through five or six feet of swirling current to get to the fish. Another place to fish a sinking-tip line is in the middle of a wide, deep pool where covering a lot of water with a floating line and indicator would be fruitless. In either case, getting a dead drift is almost impossible and you'd have to hope that the trout would be inclined to chase a swinging fly.

Double-taper or weight-forward? Use whatever you have on your current rod and whatever you're comfortable using. If you plan on buying a line especially for nymph fishing, I'd pick either a double-taper or long-belly weight-forward because these lines mend easier in tricky currents. But most nymph fishing is done with the first 30 feet or less of line where the design of the weight-forward and double-taper are nearly identical.

Use whatever color fly line strikes your fancy. Bright colors are easier to follow, especially if you plan to do some delicate nymphing without a strike indicator. Don't worry about bright lines spooking fish; besides, in clear, shallow water you should be using a long leader and presenting the fly so the line never passes over the fish. If the water is fast and deep and you need to cast over the fish to get your fly down, they're not going to notice the line. I should mention that in New Zealand, however, where they stalk big trout in transparent water, guides feel that even false casting behind fish with a bright line flashing in the sun will spook them. So if you plan to fish in New Zealand or anyplace where big trout are exposed in clear shallows, you might consider a dull gray line.

LEADERS AND TIPPETS

The leaders you use for dry-fly fishing will be fine for nymph fishing. Just make sure you carry spools of tippet material in Sizes 2X through 7X so you'll be able to modify leaders while standing on the riverbank. I almost always start with a standard knotless nylon leader, 9 feet long and tapered to 4X or 5X. With this leader I can cut it shorter for big stonefly nymphs, add a longer tippet for difficult currents and deeper water, or add a section of 6X or 7X tippet material when fishing tiny midge larvae. As you'll see in the techniques section, I like long tippets, and that 9-foot leader often grows to 15 feet in short order.

I don't think it matters whether you use modern knotless leaders or older knotted tapered leaders, although the knotted ones pick up bits of weed in spring creeks and tailwaters which hinders both your casting and presentation. Braided-butt leaders are also very useful for nymph fishing because the more supple braid presents less resistance to the current, helping you avoid drag and letting your fly sink deeper. Whatever type of leader you use, try to keep the butt section of the leader floating, or at least that part of the leader between the end of the fly line and your strike indicator. It's much easier to mend line and the heavier part of your leader if they're floating. You may need to add paste fly flotant or line dressing to your leader butt to keep it floating high. Avoid PVDF (fluorocarbon or Mirage) leader butts because PVDF is denser than nylon and hard to keep on the surface, even when dressed.

On the other hand, PVDF makes better tippets than nylon for nymph fishing. Besides the density, PVDF has a refractive index closer to water than nylon, so it almost disappears in water. And finally, PVDF is more abrasion-resistant than nylon, which is helpful when your tippet ticks across abrasive rocks on every cast. Experienced anglers whose opinion I value tell me they prefer nylon over PVDF because it is much stronger or knots better than PVDF. I've seen too many instances where PVDF has made the difference between success and failure that I'm willing to live

PVDF makes the best tippets for nymph fishing.

with the slight break-strength advantage nylon may have over PVDF in the same diameter.

To make the ideal all-around nymph leader, in my opinion, start with a knotless 9-foot, 4X nylon leader and add between 24 and 40 inches of 5X PVDF tippet.

WEIGHT

Unless trout are feeding on nymphs in the surface film or in water less than a foot deep, you'll need some help getting your fly to their level. Weight can be incorporated into the fly as part of the dressing, using either a wire underbody or a metal bead. Weight can also be added to the leader. There is a minor controversy among nymph fishers as to which is more natural and more effective. One camp believes an unweighted nymph at the end of the tippet behaves more naturally, so they use all unweighted flies and apply split shot or other weights to the leader. The theory here is that an unweighted nymph swings freely in the current below the point where the weight is attached to the leader. Another school of thought says that a tippet always hinders the action of a nymph because both nylon and

PVDF are fairly stiff materials (compared to thread or a rubber band in the same diameter), and weight added to a fly counteracts this stiffness. I lean toward the second school myself, but in experiments I've done using nymphs fished both ways I have not seen any measurable difference in effectiveness.

The biggest advantage of having at least some of your flies tied weighted comes when sight-fishing to trout where a strike indicator and split shot on the leader may spook the fish. In this case, you want to pitch your fly slightly upstream of the trout's position and get it down to your quarry as quickly as possible. Weight on the leader not only makes a big splash, but the sight of a string of shiny split shot close to your fly may warn a spooky trout that something is not quite right.

Weighted Flies

Flies tied with wire underneath the dressing sink the slowest and are best for shallow water or when using additional weight on the leader. Flies used to be weighted with lead, but lead in the water has proven to be a health risk for waterfowl and some companies, notably Orvis, have taken the position that no flies or split shot they sell will contain lead. (Weighted flies sold by Orvis are now tied with tin wire, which is not as heavy as lead but still adds weight to the dressing.) In Vermont, after ponds and lakes freeze over, the black ducks and mallards pour into our trout streams. I've watched these ducks scour riffles for hours, presumably grubbing for caddis larvae. Why take the

A brass or tungsten bead on the head of a fly will increase its sink rate.

chance that a mallard might ingest a leaded fly or piece of split shot you lost on the bottom?

If you want more weight, choose a fly with a brass bead or two incorporated into the dressing. Beads pack more weight onto a fly, and a nymph tied with a single brass bead sinks twice as fast as a fly weighted with tin wire. A tungsten bead of the same diameter sinks about three times as fast as a standard weighted fly, and you can regulate your fly's depth just by changing patterns. For instance, the famous Prince Nymph is available with a standard wire underbody, with a brass bead (Bead-Head Prince), or with a tungsten bead (Tung-head Prince). If you find trout feeding in a shallow flat with their fins practically out of the water, you'd use the standard fly; when fishing a three-foot-deep riffle

Tungsten, Brass, & Unweighted Sink Rates in Inches per Second

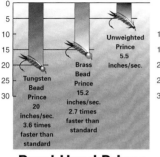

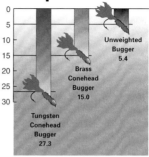

Bead-Head Prince Sink Rates

Conehead Woolly Bugger Sink Rates

Comparison of sink rates of different types of flies.

you'd go to the Bead-Head version to get your fly closer to the fish; and in a very fast, deep run, the Tunghead flavor would be most effective.

Adding Weight to the Leader

Of course, you could accomplish the same thing by adding weight to the leader. The most popular method is to pinch from one to a half-dozen split shot to the leader. Non-toxic split shot made of a tin alloy is available, and although it's not as heavy as lead, it crimps easily to a leader with forceps or pliers. Removable versions, with a tiny slit opposite the side the leader slips into, are available. Split shot is widely available

Sink Putty and tin shot of about the same weight. Note that it takes three shot to equal the weight of the tungsten putty. Also note the rounded shape of the putty, which stays on better than a torpedo shape.

and familiar to most anglers, but it can damage a fine tippet and even the removable type is tricky to put on and take off.

Other weights include "twist-ons," thin strips of lead you wrap around the leader, and my favorite, Sink Putty. The putty is made from tungsten powder combined with an adhesive. It is heavier than lead, non-toxic, can be removed in seconds, and you can add or subtract lumps of putty to regulate the weight on your leader with a precision not possible with any other kind of material. If it gets caught on the bottom, it can also be pulled from a snag much easier than a string of hard split shot.

I frequently hear complaints from anglers that Sink Putty won't stay on the leader or that it slips down against the fly during casting. There are a couple of tricks to prevent this. First, pre-stretch the tippet before adding any putty. Next, take a small amount of putty between your fingertips and rub it back and forth along the tippet in the spot you want to add weight until the leader takes on a dull gray film of putty. Now stretch the tippet, roll on the putty, and then relax the tippet. You'll seldom have a problem with your weight slipping. (Be careful that there is no slippery fly or line dressing on the tippet—these will make the weight slip and there's no solution except to replace the tippet and start over.)

One final trick to using Sink Putty: Resist the urge to roll it onto the leader in a slim, streamlined shape. It won't cast much easier, and the leader slips out of the thin ends, giving you a weight that spins in the water and will fall off the leader in short order. An egg shape will last much longer and sink quicker because it offers less resistance in the water.

INDICATORS

You may be surprised to learn there was nymph fishing before strike indicators. When I started nymph fishing more than 35 years ago, your indicator was the tip of your floating line. It was truly a mystical art, because detecting strikes this way takes practice and not a small amount of intuition. A master, Carl D. Coleman, taught me his technique, which was to fish a heavily leaded fly (this was also before the days of Bead-Heads) straight upstream on a heavy tippet. The first time he took me fishing, I was astounded to see him take a half-dozen big, wild brown trout from a run that didn't even look like it would hold a seven-incher. I now realize that his success was due as much to his intimate knowledge of that stretch of water as it was his technique or fly pattern, but I doubt if I could have learned the technique from a book.

Strike indicators started life as just that—things stuck to your leader that showed you all those subtle takes you were missing by just watching the line. It takes a quick, deliberate strike in relatively fast water to move the tip of a floating line. Later, fly fishers realized that a strike indicator was just as valuable in telling you how and where your fly was drifting.

Stick-On Indicators

These are pieces of plastic foam with adhesive backs that you fold over the tippet. Novices often use them because they appear to be the easiest to use. Avoid them. They can't be moved once you stick them on the leader, they leave a sticky residue once you get them off, and they aren't reusable. Foam indicators are also a major source of non-biodegradable litter on some rivers.

Hard-Bodied Indicators

Indicators made from balsa wood, cork, or plastic last for years, float without added dressing, seldom slip off the leader, and are easy to see. Some are threaded onto the tippet and jammed in place with a twig or toothpick, others twist on the leader with rubber grommets hidden inside the indicator or are kept in place with a piece of rubber tubing. They are easy to move up and down the tippet according to water depth, but most have to be threaded on the tippet, so you have to remove your fly and weight before adding one to the leader. They come in sizes from very tiny for delicate fishing with midge pupae to giant ones that rival bobbers used for live-bait fishing. The biggest ones are particularly useful when fishing giant stonefly nymphs and lots of lead on the leader because they suspend the fly and are almost unsinkable. Needless to say, the real big ones are not pretty to cast.

Yarn Indicators

These rival the hard-bodied indicators in floating qualities, although they need line dressing or dry-fly flotant to keep them floating all day long. They are the most sensitive indicators known, and are particularly good in cold or slow water where strikes are so tentative they might be missed with other kinds of indicators. Yarn indicators stick up high above the water so they are visible even in boiling white water. They are also less wind-resistant and easier to cast.

Yarn indicators come in many types. The simplest is a piece of polypropylene yarn (poly yarn is lighter than water) looped onto the tippet with a slip knot. It's cheap and you can easily regulate the size of your indicator. Another type comes as a pre-made indicator

Strike indicators. From left to right: A large piece of Strike Putty for fishing fast water, a small piece of Strike Putty for shallow water or sight fishing, a yarn indicator looped on the leader with an O-ring, a hard-bodied foam indicator, and a clip-on yarn indicator.

with an O-ring or loop at one end, which is slip-knotted to the leader without removing the fly from the tippet. The easiest style of yarn indicator to use has a plastic spring clip at one end; the leader fits into a slot on the plastic piece, and you can clip the indicator to the leader, remove it, or move it from one place to another on your leader in about five seconds.

Strike Putty

Like Sink Putty, this buoyant, reusable material is versatile because you can regulate the size of your indicator. It comes as a lump in a plastic tub, and you pinch off what you need and roll it onto your tippet. Suppose you're fishing a fast, deep riffle, with a pea-sized lump of Sink Putty on your tippet to get the fly down, and a lump of Strike Putty as big as a marble on the butt section of your leader. Approaching the tail of the next pool, you spot several big trout nymphing in the shallows. Simply strip the Sink Putty off your tippet and leave all but a tiny spot of Strike Putty on the leader—too small to splash when it hits, so it won't spook the fish, yet visible enough to let you know if a trout grabs the nymph.

Indicator Colors

Most indicators come in shades of red, orange, yellow, or chartreuse. Red and orange are best in bright sunlight, in white water, and over light-colored bottoms; yellow and chartreuse seem most visible in the shade, in the evening, over dark bottoms, and on cloudy days. From underneath, all of them probably look the same to the fish because of backlighting, so experiment and pick the one that's easiest for you to spot.

Dry-Fly Indicators

Many fishermen use a high-floating, easily spotted dry fly as an indicator. This offers major advantages: It provides the opportunity to catch a fish on a dry fly (which is always fun); it allows you to prospect for trout with two entirely different types of flies at different levels; and the dry fly may also act as an attractor. Trout often rise to look at a dry but may turn away at the last minute. On the way down, they may see an easier meal in the nymph and grab it. Because trout can see stuff floating on the surface from farther away

Indicator dries should be highly visible and buoyant. The Stimulator is a big favorite with Rocky Mountain guides.

than they can a submerged object, it truly increases the chances that they'll see your nymph.

It's amazing how quickly a trout can refuse a dry fly and then quickly inhale a nymph. Countless times I've seen a trout rise to my dry, set the hook, and found the nymph firmly hooked in the fish's mouth when I landed it!

The best dry flies to use as indicators are those that float high through numerous casts and dousings. For the early season, use high-floating imitations of stone-flies like the Stimulator, buoyant caddisflies like the Irresistible Caddis, or large mayfly imitations with visible white wings like the Hare's-Ear Parachute. During the summer months, the best indicators are imitations of terrestrial insects like foam beetles or grasshoppers. The disadvantage of using dry flies as indicators is that they are never as easy to follow in the current as a fluorescent piece of cork or yarn, nor do they float as well.

CHAPTER 3

NYMPH FISHING TECHNIQUES

Don't ever fool yourself into thinking you'll make your fly look like a naturally drifting nymph for more than a few feet. With the average 30-foot cast, your fly will behave exactly like a drifting natural for two or three feet, sort of like a natural for 15 feet, and completely wrong for the other 12 feet. Don't lose any sleep over this. Just as you'll never buy or tie a fly that looks exactly like a mayfly, you'll never get the perfect drift. But trout aren't very bright, and pretty close is good enough to fool them.

Fish can be amazingly fussy about the speed and depth of their prey, even if the fly pattern is right. Everything you do in nymph presentation should strive to keep your fly at a trout's level as long as possible and at a speed that does not arouse suspicion. With the exception of some caddis pupae, scuds, and swimming mayfly nymphs, most insects drift at the mercy of the current, with an occasional wiggle of their bodies that makes them rise in the current, followed by a period of rest where they sink or stay suspended in the water column. You can't imitate this wiggle—forget about it. The bobbing of a strike indicator in choppy water, however, may cause your fly to rise and fall gently in the water, a benefit of strike indicators that is often overlooked.

Most of the time the trout are within a foot of the bottom where current speed is slow enough to let them maintain their positions without working too hard. They will move for a fly anywhere from a few inches to a few feet, depending on water temperature, clarity, and the amount of food in the water. Most times they won't move up more than about eight inches (or they may not be able to see a fly farther because of bubbles or turbidity in the water). It's important to get your fly close to the bottom—but obviously not *on* the bottom. Besides the fact that you'll hang up on the bottom, disturbing the water and losing lots of flies, trout never

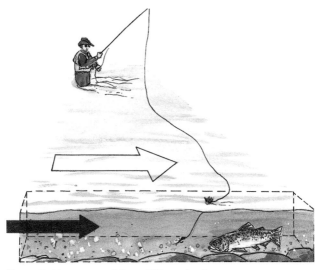

Forces that keep a nymph from drifting naturally.

eat things drifting *under* them *because they can't see them.* Almost none of their feeding is done by grubbing *on* the bottom, because they have to tip their bodies tail-up, which wastes energy. Plucking food from the drift is far more efficient.

When dry-fly fishing, drag is any pull from the line or leader that makes the fly move contrary to the current, whether it's upstream, downstream, or across-stream. Drag-free drifts are just as critical in nymph fishing, but the fly can move slightly upstream or downstream (imitating that rising and falling motion) as long as it does not move across currents. Once you cast your fly, imagine a vertical lane from the surface to the bottom parallel to the direction of the current. As long as your fly drifts along this lane, close enough for trout lying near the bottom to see it, you should be able to tease some of them into eating your nymph.

WET-FLY SWING

Casting a fly across the current and letting it swing below you is the least cumbersome, least scientific—and probably the least productive—way of fishing nymphs. However, it can be deadly when insects are actively hatching and you see a few scattered rises in a pool. It does not work with a strike indicator, and weight on the leader hinders its effectiveness. The fly is cast quartering upstream about 45 degrees, followed by a quick upstream mend. As the fly drifts downstream, tension is put on its drift by the line and leader because the currents at the surface are always faster

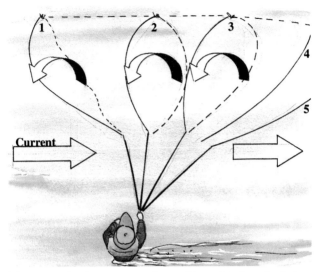

When quartering downstream, make careful mends to keep the fly from skittering across the river.

than below. The line and leader begin to belly downstream, pulling the fly out of that vertical lane, sweeping it across the current faster that the natural flow.

There are ways to arrest the cross-current progress of the fly. One is to make frequent small mends in the line. Reach straight out over the water, point the rod tip at the fly, and flip a small loop of line upstream. Try not to move the line lying on the surface, nor the fly or leader, when you mend. It's natural for a drifting nymph to rise and fall slightly in the water column, but any movement you make with your clumsy arms is way out of proportion to the distance a natural fly can move. When some species of caddisflies or swimming mayflies are hatching, purposely moving the fly with mends can draw smashing strikes, but most times it does more harm than good.

In combination with mends (or instead of mends), try following the suspected position of the fly with the rod tip, keeping as much line as possible off the water by raising the rod tip to slow a fly's sideways skid. And notice I said the suspected position of *the fly,* not where the line enters the water. This technique works better with short casts; with a 50-foot cast, it's tough to keep enough line off the water to affect the fly's drift.

The wet-fly swing works best with an unweighted or lightly weighted fly. Of course, it is the method of choice for fishing traditional winged or soft-hackle wet flies. These flies are tied on heavy hooks with soft, water-absorbent materials that sink quickly without added weight, and have lifelike mobility in the water. Traditional nymphs can be used as well. I've had better luck with soft, fuzzy nymphs like the Hare's-Ear or hackled nymphs like the Zug Bug than I have with stiffer, harder flies like most stonefly imitations.

The wet-fly swing works better in slow to moderate currents than it does in very fast or broken water. It's a great way to cover the middle or tail of a large pool when you have no idea where the trout are; trying to fish a 100-foot-wide pool with an indicator and split shot might wear you out before you hook a fish! In smooth water like this, use at least a 9-foot leader or preferably a 12-footer. Your fly will sink with less hindrance because these leaders have longer tippets (thinner nylon has less resistance in the water), and you'll be keeping the heavy fly line farther from spooky flat-water trout.

UPSTREAM WITH NO INDICATOR

I learned to fish nymphs without the benefit of strike indicators (they have only been widely used since about 1980), and I still love to fish that way if conditions allow. Sight-fishing to spooky fish in shallow water is best done without a bulky indicator because the splash of an indicator often scares trout, but there are

When fishing directly upstream, standing in the same current lane the fly is drifting through will give you a drag-free presentation.

other places you can fish effectively without a bobber stuck onto your leader. Generally, the shallower the water and the more aggressively fish feed, the easier it is to catch them without an indicator. It's also better where currents are relatively uniform—tricky pocket water full of swirls really screams for a strike indicator.

Direct Upstream Approach

Let's say there's a caddis hatch on the water, you see a few splashy rises in a fast riffle, but the fish won't touch a dry fly. Here's a perfect opportunity to try a weighted caddis pupa or Bead-Head. Cast straight upstream or slightly across-and-upstream, just as you would with a dry. It helps if your tippet collapses a bit to get the fly below the surface before the leader begins to pull it to the surface. A great trick is to employ Joe Humphreys's famous Tuck Cast. This cast drives the fly into the water and piles some of the leader di-

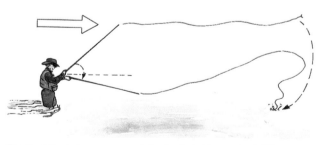

The Tuck Cast gives your nymph the best start to a natural drift.

rectly over it, giving the fly added margin for sinking. To perform the Tuck Cast, stop your forward cast higher than normal right after the forward power stroke. At the same time, tip your wrist down about 30 degrees below the horizontal. If you're doing it properly, the fly will hit the water with a splat before the line and leader.

If you are fishing directly upstream, keep the rod tip low and strip in line as the current gathers it to you. Strikes will appear to make the line jump upstream, or the leader might tighten, or a curl in the butt section of the leader might straighten. It's not black magic as many anglers would have you believe—set the hook if the line or leader do anything that looks like they are not just drifting with the current. You can hone your technique if you can find some whitefish, chubs, shiners, or bluegills. These fish take nymphs readily and hold onto a fake insect longer than trout.

When fishing directly upstream, try to stand in the same current lane as the water you're fishing and don't mend line. Mending line without an indicator on the leader makes the fly move unnaturally, no matter how carefully you mend. Everything needs to be done before the fly hits the water with either a Tuck Cast or a sloppy slack-line cast. Casting directly upstream has the disadvantage of putting the line and leader directly over a trout's head, especially if you misjudge a cast. Therefore, it works best in very fast water where the splash of a fly line hitting the water may be ignored over the noise of a riffle.

High-Sticking

The biggest disadvantage of fishing directly up-stream with a floating line is that the current is always faster at the surface than down below because friction with the bottom of the river slows the water's velocity. As soon as your cast hits the water, the fly line and leader move downstream faster than the sunken fly. This is why the Tuck Cast is so effective—it both drives your fly down toward the bottom and adds some slack above the fly. The fly has a chance to sink before the line draws it downstream and up through the water column. This effect is accentuated if you're casting to the eddy behind a rock or against the far bank and your line falls on a faster current close to you.

A more typical situation than standing in the same current lane as the fly is when you are standing in the slower, shallower water near shore and you want to fish your nymph in deeper water closer to the center of the river. If the current you're standing in is slower than where you want to drift your nymph, the fly line will bow upstream while the nymph drifts past, quickly forming a whiplash effect, making the fly jerk upstream. If the current you are standing in is faster, the line will tow the fly downstream. You might argue that action like this makes the fly appear to be rising to the surface like a hatching nymph. This might be at-tractive to a trout under certain conditions, but take my word for it—95 percent of the time you'll get more strikes if your fly is drifting just as fast as the current.

High-sticking the edge of a deep run. Note the very short cast, helpful in maintaining line control.

One solution is to keep most or all of the fly line off the water by holding the rod tip high, a method developed in Colorado known as "high-sticking." The method works best with short casts, usually under 30 feet, and is ideally suited to fast, swirling pocket water where trout aren't too spooky and you can get very close to them. Stand just opposite to a place where you think a trout might be feeding. Cast upstream and a little beyond this spot to allow the fly to sink to a trout's level. How far above the fish's position you cast depends upon the depth of the water and the amount of weight on your fly and leader. In three feet of water with a moderate current, with a bead-head fly on your leader, cast about 10 feet upstream and two feet to the other side of its suspected position. With weight on the leader or a Tuck Cast, you can cut that lead in half.

Two-Fly Rigs

Regardless of whether you try the methods above or the indicator fishing techniques to follow, you may want to fish with two nymphs at once. The advantages are obvious—you get to try two different patterns to see which one the fish prefer, and your flies drift at slightly different levels. Before you get too excited, though, a word of warning: Where snags are frequent, you'll lose two flies at a time as opposed to one, and when it's windy this arrangement is on a par with a root canal. Tangles are frequent, so be patient.

The most common two-fly arrangement is to add the second fly by tying it to the bend or eye of the first fly.

Size 14 Bead–Head Prince Nymph

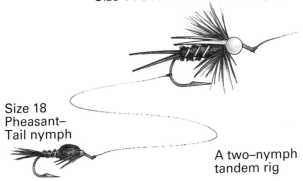
Size 18
Pheasant–
Tail nymph

A two–nymph
tandem rig

Two-fly rig. The smaller fly could also be attached to the eye of the larger fly with a clinch knot.

For instance, let's say you're fishing a Size 12 Hare's-Ear Nymph on a 4X tippet and want to try something smaller and in a different color. Tie a 12-inch piece of 5X tippet material to the bend of your Hare's-Ear with a clinch knot, and then tie a Size 16 Green Caddis Pupa to the end of the 5X. The lower fly is typically smaller than the upper fly, and the tippet used for it is one size smaller than the main tippet.

There is a temptation to try a really large fly for the upper one and a tiny fly for the lower, but I've found this doesn't work well for reasons I can't begin to fathom. Perhaps seeing two flies of vastly different proportions does not seem natural. You'll have better luck if you don't vary the size of the two flies by more than two hook sizes. Often you'll see two flies on the water at once; for instance, a Size 14 caddis and a Size 18 mayfly. This makes your choice easy—put on imitations of corresponding size and silhouette. If there aren't any visible hatches, try the nymph most recommended for the stream in question and the same pattern two sizes smaller. If you are mixing and matching, take your best shot with the upper fly and use the lower one for experimentation.

When putting weight on the leader, it's best to put all the weight above the upper fly. You can also experiment by adding weight on the tippet between the two flies, but that arrangement has never worked well for me and it induces tangles. You might also occasionally foul hook trout when fishing two flies. What usually happens is that a trout takes the upper fly but ejects it before you set the hook. By the time you strike, the lower fly ends up in the trout's butt. You can avoid this by making the lower tippet longer (around 16 inches), and perhaps by changing the upper fly to the same pattern one size smaller.

INDICATOR FISHING

As I stated before, strike indicators have become much more than *bite* indicators. You'll also find them handy as *drift* indicators, and the bigger ones also function as drift *regulators*. I urge you to experiment with several styles, especially when you fish different water types. My vest contains at least four different types of indicators and three styles of weight at any given time.

New flavors come out every year, and I urge you to watch magazine articles and fishing catalogs for the latest varieties. The perfect indicator has yet to appear and it only costs a few bucks to try a new one.

Whatever else you do when fishing a nymph with a strike indicator, the most important part of the game is to keep the fly and indicator drifting in the same current lane, and to make sure both continue in the same current lane throughout the drift. Any way you can accomplish this, no matter how unorthodox it may seem, will make nymph fishing more productive.

Using Dry-Fly Indicators

Using a dry fly as an indicator couldn't be easier. Tie a piece of tippet to the bend of the dry-fly hook and tie a nymph to the end of the tippet. This rig will not cast as well as you think—just adding a piece of nylon and even a small nymph can do nasty things to your casting, and you'll have to sacrifice tight loops and long casts for a more relaxed style with an open loop. Also, if you're fishing heavy fast water and need weight on the leader, a dry fly won't be up to the task of suspending a pair of large weighted flies and a hunk of soft lead. But for fishing shallow riffles or slow pools, a dry-fly indicator is just right.

In my backyard flows a small trout stream full of wild and very spooky browns and rainbows with a few brookies mixed in. My favorite rig for this shallow, clear river is a Size 18 Black Caddis Pupa fished underneath a Size 14 Foam Beetle. The tippet to the bee-

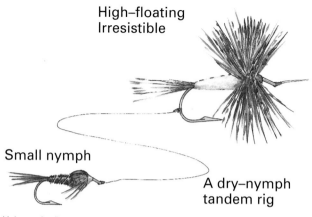

High–floating
Irresistible

Small nymph

A dry–nymph
tandem rig

Using a dry fly as a strike indicator.

tle is about three feet of 6X and the nymph is separated
from the dry by two feet of 7X. I can't cast more than
40 feet with these flies, but it seldom spooks trout and
I catch fish on both the beetle and the nymph.

Cast upstream with a slight Tuck Cast so the nymph
enters the water first. Watch the dry fly's progress as it
floats back to you. Avoid drag as you would fishing a
single dry, and if you see the floater hesitate or bob
slightly, set the hook quickly but not viciously. Enough
tightening to move the dry fly a few inches will be
enough force to set the hook. If a trout splashes at the
dry but does not take it, watch the fly carefully as
many fish drop back and take the nymph.

Silicate dry-fly desiccant, a white powder sold under
names such as Dry Flotant, is invaluable when using a

dry-fly indicator. When your dry becomes hard to spot, grind it into a small amount of this miracle powder and blow on the fly until most of the powder is removed. This process removes moisture from the dry and coats it with a layer of hydrophobic silicone powder.

For most riffles, two feet of tippet between the dry and the nymph is about right. If there are insects hatching and you see an occasional rise, the distance between the two can be as short as a foot. But this technique is also deadly in deep, slow water where takes are so subtle that sometimes a standard indicator won't register the strike. In a pool over three feet deep, use about five feet of tippet between the nymph and the dry. Warning: This rig is harder to cast than it seems. Your casting will feel clumsy, even if both nymph and dry are quite small. But the rewards are often worth the effort.

Using Foam and Yarn Indicators

Foam and yarn indicators have made nymph fishing a technique that even first-time fly fishers can understand and use effectively. An experienced guide in a drift boat can rig up an angler who has never held a fly rod with a pair of nymphs and some weight on the leader, plus a high-floating indicator, and have the client catch scores of trout in a single day. The guide keeps the boat drifting even with the indicator, and can often fish through 50 yards of water without even mending the line; all the angler has to do is set the hook. Some anglers look down on this kind of fishing, calling it bobber fishing. Make your own decision and don't be intimidated by self-righteous "experts." There are times when only a big indicator with weight will interest trout, and most of us would rather play a few trout in a day of fishing than not.

I'll assume that most of your fishing will be on your own where you won't have the benefit of a guide's prudent advice and accomplished boat-handling skills. The best advice I can give you about indicator fishing is to pick a flexible arrangement. If you can quickly move the indicator up and down the leader, and add, subtract, or move the weight, you'll spend more time fishing and less time fussing with tackle.

A Typical Scenario

The best rig for fast currents and water over two feet deep is a clip-on yarn indicator and tungsten Sink Putty for weight (if needed). Let's say you're starting out in a moderate riffle in the middle of a pool, with current about as fast as a walk and two feet deep. You have a 9-foot, 5X leader, and you know the fish in this river like a Size 14 Bead-Head Prince Nymph. Without a lot of weight on the leader, your fly will invariably drift at an angle to the indicator, not directly below it. A rule of thumb is to set the indicator at twice the depth of the water, so tie on the nymph and clip the strike indicator four feet up the leader.

If the fly is weighted and you don't have a strike in two dozen casts and notice the indicator has never hesitated, you are probably fishing nowhere near the bot-

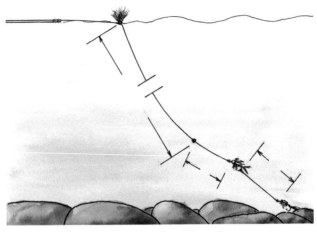

The most common way to fish nymphs with an indicator.

tom. It takes far more weight than you might think to get the fly close to the fish. The fly might also be dragging unnaturally because the indicator at the surface is drifting much faster than the nymph below. To slow down the fly and get it deeper, roll a piece of Sink Putty half the size of a pea to the tippet a foot above the fly. The weight will get the fly deeper and help slow it down as it drifts.

If you still don't get any sign of hesitation in the indicator, add enough Sink Putty to the original clump to increase its size about 30 percent. Now, every half-dozen casts the indicator hesitates slightly, as if the fly were ticking along the bottom. Each time you set the hook but there is no weight at the other end. Another few casts and the indicator hesitates more decisively—set the hook and land and release a nice rainbow.

Since adding some weight increased your success, you decide to add more. Now you double the size of the lump of Sink Putty, and on every cast the indicator hesitates. After a few more casts it really stops dead and you are firmly attached to a rock on the streambed. You've learned two important lessons. First, when you find the right combination of weight and indicator setting, don't change a thing. Second, it's possible to be too close to the bottom. Not only will you hang up frequently and lose many flies, but the trout may be missing your fly because it's drifting too deep. Remember, they may be close to the bottom but they feed on stuff drifting *above* the bottom.

You decide to move closer to the head of the pool where the water is deeper—about four feet. You make a dozen casts and suspect the fly is not getting deep enough as it never hesitates. Instead of adding weight, you move the strike indicator four feet closer to the fly line to match the water's depth. You also make a more pronounced Tuck Cast, putting more authority into the downward flick of your wrist. The combination of the increased depth of the indicator and the Tuck Cast is enough to drift your nymph at the right level, and you take another small rainbow and a frisky, butter-colored 14-inch brown trout. Equal success might have come from adding more weight to the leader, but casting and fishing are more pleasant if you can get to the same place without additional weight.

Ways to Get the Fly Deeper and Avoid Drag

Avoiding unnatural drag and getting the fly deeper go hand-in-hand. You have a number of arrows in your quiver of techniques:

- **Cast at an angle closer to directly upstream.** Any time you cast off to one side, the current will pull the indicator and line directly downstream faster than the nymph. It will also pull them to one side, toward you and the tip of the rod.
- **Add more weight to the leader.** Adding weight— about 30 percent at a time—seems to be about right. When the indicator hesitates at the end of the drift, bumping bottom every three or four casts just before the line straightens, your nymph should be drifting about right.
- **Move the indicator closer to the fly line.** Make sure it's somewhere around twice the depth of the water (unless you have a very heavy chunk of Sink Putty). If you've pushed the envelope in weight, the indicator can be set to slightly less than the water depth.
- **Use a Tuck Cast.** It's an extremely useful technique that helps the fly drift deeper and free of drag.
- **Use a Post-Cast Tuck.** I have never seen this used or described before, but it works for me. After the fly and indicator hit the water, lift your rod tip sharply while pointing it straight at the indicator. This lifts the line and indicator, giving the nymph some slack to sink, and the nymph and weight

pivot around the indicator, driving them deeper. It's like a mend but you are not moving the fly line to one side or the other.

- **Make an upstream mend.** Similar to the technique above, throw a loop of fly line upstream of the indicator. Try to do this without moving the indicator so you don't make the nymph jump like a grasshopper caught on a hot sidewalk.

- **Make shorter casts and hold the rod tip high.** The longer you cast, the harder it is to control the fly and indicator. Keep casts short, as in the high-sticking method, while keeping most or all of the line and leader above the indicator off the water. It is a deadly way to fish fast, deep water, if you can wade close enough.

- **Lengthen Your Tippet.** The finer the connection between the leader butt and the nymph, the less resistance the leader offers to the water and the faster the fly can sink—and the more naturally it will drift. Adding more tippet material can give you a deeper, more natural drift; four feet of 5X instead of two feet can dramatically increase your success.

When Deeper Isn't Better

Usually, you'll be fishing too shallow if you don't pay attention to the amount of weight and the setting of your indicator. There are times, however, when you'll want a nymph to drift higher in the water column. Early in the morning and in the evening, it's hard for a trout to see your fly when it's close to the bottom. Try moving the indicator closer to the fly until it's at the water's depth or even half the depth. Setting the indicator so the fly rides higher can also make a difference during a hatch when insects are rising toward the surface.

Extending the Drift

Despite your best efforts, at some point the line between your rod tip will tighten, pulling the nymph and indicator toward you and the surface. This usually happens right after the fly is at its deepest and most drag-free position—most often as it drifts past where you're

Extending the downstream drift of a nymph. Note the angler feeding line and the rod tip pointed at the indicator.

standing. You will catch most trout just before this spot, but there are ways to get a longer drift and cover more water with each cast. Sometimes just lifting the rod will extend the drift. Follow the indicator with the tip of the rod, and hold the rod high but horizontally above the indicator. On longer casts, it's difficult to raise the rod without pulling the indicator toward you. In this situation, you can mend a large loop of slack line upstream and beyond the indicator. As the indicator floats downstream, keep the rod tip pointing at the indicator. Feed line into the loop by wiggling the rod tip gently from side to side while letting slack line slip through the guides. The loop absorbs the slight movements of the rod tip, so the indicator and the fly don't move. Keep feeding slack until the indicator starts to slide sideways. At this point there is nothing else you can do except let the fly and indicator hang below you in preparation for the next cast.

Sometimes trout strike when the line tightens and the fly rises toward the surface. This usually happens when there is an insect hatch and they are chasing emerging flies to the surface. It seems like this would be a natural movement and a prime time for strikes, but it happens less often than you might think.

At times, wading conditions or snags along a bank may make it impossible to fish any way but directly downstream. This is a far tougher way to fish, and trout are more likely spooked when you are above them. Still, if it's the only way to get your nymph into position, cast downstream with a serious slack-line cast by overpowering the cast and stopping it short, so line, leader, and fly land in a pile. Immediately start feeding slack into the drift (as if you were extending a normal drift). Strikes will be even more subtle than usual, so set the hook at the slightest hesitation of the indicator.

When fishing a rig with lots of weight on the leader, casting is difficult, dangerous, and clumsy. The best way to make another cast and reposition the fly for the next drift is to wait until the line, indicator, and fly hang directly downstream. Extend the rod tip all the way back until it points directly at the indicator, then sling the whole thing back upstream by moving the rod tip in a broad, quick arc. The line hanging in the water will load the rod and there is no need to make a false cast. With no false casts, you are less likely to tangle the leader, and less likely to skim your ear with a big chunk of tungsten. Another trick is to move the rod tip to one side or another just at the completion of this up-stream lob. This movement creates an upstream loop that will give you a longer, deeper drift.

Other Ways to Rig Indicators

The clip-on yarn and Sink Putty rig described previously is the most flexible arrangement, and it allows you to instantly switch to a dry fly if trout begin feeding on the surface. Alternatively, you can use a yarn indicator with a rubber O-ring or slip-knot a piece of yarn to the leader butt. With most cork and foam indicators, fishing techniques are the same, but to add or remove them you must remove all flies and weight from the leader because the leader gets threaded up the middle of these.

Big, extremely buoyant plastic or cork indicators come into their own when you want to suspend a heavily weighted rig in deep, fast water. Yarn is not buoyant enough to hold a big stonefly nymph plus two peanut-sized chunks of weight off the bottom. When water is over five feet deep and very fast, especially with strong turbulence that tosses your fly around like a milkweed seed on a fall day, no cast is long enough to sink the fly. Here you must get your nymph down *right now* and under control. The only way is to attach as much weight to the leader as you can sling, with an indicator that will hold it just above the bottom.

One of the most difficult places to fish nymphs is in swirling currents where your leader and indicator are pulled in many directions and it's difficult to tell if your nymph is drifting at the same speed as the indicator. Strikes are also tough to detect. A double-strike-indicator technique I learned from guides in Colorado makes these conditions much easier to handle. Place one strike indicator where you normally would, at about twice the depth of the water from the fly. Then add a second indicator two feet above the first one. Mend line so that both indicators form a straight line, pointing toward the place you think your fly is drifting. Keep mending as the fly drifts toward you. This avoids arcs in the leader that can cause drag.

In fact, this double-indicator method is great for novice nymph fishers in any current; it's easier to follow the progress of the fly than with a single indicator, and it teaches them about drag caused by loops in the line.

Strike Putty is wonderful stuff for the double-indicator method because it's not as important that the indicators float as high when you have two of them. I also use Strike Putty with unweighted flies and leaders such as when fishing tiny Pheasant-Tail Nymphs in shallow riffles. However, when fishing with weight on the leader or where it's tough to keep the fly and indicator in the same current lane, Strike Putty is not as effective as a yarn or foam indicator. A round ball of Strike Putty offers little resistance to the pull of the line or leader butt, so it gives a drifting nymph little defense against drag.

One final strike indicator setup is the Right-Angle Nymph Rig (or Suspension Rig) developed in California. It places the tippet and fly at right angles to the indicator and helps them drift deeper, suspended under the indicator. Start with a short, heavy leader, about 7½ feet long and ending at no lighter than 2X. The end of the leader can be even heavier for big flies and stiff winds. At the end of the leader, attach a yarn strike indicator with a clinch knot. You can either knot the leader to the rubber O-ring of a pre-made indicator or knot it to the center of a loose bunch of floating yarn.

Use a clinch knot to tie a tippet about equal to the depth of the water either to the O-ring or to the end of the leader. The tippet is usually 4X or 5X material, depending on the size of the fly and clarity of the water. Lighter tippets can be effective but they tangle easily. You'll notice the tippet and the fly at its end come off

Right-Angle Nymph Rig.

from the indicator at a right angle, so once the rig hits the water the fly is forced toward the bottom quicker than if it were on one continuous length. This arrangement gives great drifts, but it's difficult to cast and you must rebuild or replace your entire leader if you want to change to a dry fly.

Other Ways to Fish Weight and Multiple Flies

In the examples above, we've been looking at a single fly and weight on the tippet about a foot from the fly. The nymph can be weighted or unweighted depending upon the depth and speed of the water. I prefer to try a weighted nymph with no lead on the leader first because I feel it's more natural and easier to cast. As I stated earlier, some anglers feel an unweighted fly looks more natural, but I don't agree. I'll often change from a lightly weighted nymph (tied with a wire underbody) to one with a brass bead to get deeper. Finally, I'll try a fly with a tungsten bead head before adding weight to the leader.

Instead of putting Sink Putty or split shot directly on the tippet, you can place it on a dropper tied above the fly. Here you leave a 2-inch-long tag end of the blood knot used to attach the tippet (the heavier tag is better). Attach the weight to this tag dropper. The advantage here is that if the weight hangs up, you'll lose just the lead but not the tippet and fly. I've also seen rigs where you put the weight on the end of the tippet and put the fly on the dropper. With this rig, the weight should bump along the bottom and the fly should ride just above. This makes perfect sense, but I've seen it mostly in magazines. I've tried it and found it to be no better or worse than putting the weight above the fly. None of my friends use it, so maybe that tells you something.

Fishing a second lower fly—typically a smaller one on a lighter tippet—seems to work best with weight only above the upper fly (with no additional weight between the two flies). This keeps the lower fly actually drifting higher in the water column than the upper fly because current welling up from the bottom pulls it up. However, if the water is cold or very fast and you suspect the trout are glued to the bottom, you might try adding a smaller amount of weight between the two flies. This keeps both of them close to the bottom, but it also makes casting tougher and tangles more frequent.

SIGHT-FISHING

Being able to see your quarry makes any kind of fishing more complex—and more exciting. Flats fishing for bonefish, casting to tailing redfish, pursuing breaking stripers in the surf, dry-fly fishing during a hatch—all bring visual stimulation to a level surpassed by few things in life, plus they add to the primordial satisfaction of the stalk. Sight fishing with a nymph is no exception.

Sight-fishing is usually done in shallow water and in streams with lots of food like spring creeks and tailwaters. It's tough to see trout in deep water, and more difficult to gauge their reactions. And because the buffet line of food is constricted into a narrow vertical range in shallow water, trout are more likely to feed in the shallows than in relatively sterile deep water. Despite being in water just deep enough to cover their shoulders, sight

Sight-fishing in a rich tailwater—in this case, Colorado's Frying Pan.

fishing is best in shallow streams with lots of food because trout get preoccupied with feeding and are less spooky. And the more frequently they feed, the more likely they'll make a mistake and inhale your fraud.

Sight fishing requires careful observation of the water from as far away as possible. Even binoculars can be helpful. The fish themselves are difficult to spot; look instead for their shadows, which are much darker and more distinct. Also watch for the gentle swaying motion of a trout's tail.

The best setup is a trout in very shallow riffles that is actively moving from side to side. In shallow water, trout see very little of the world above, and the riffles mask the landing of your leader and fly on the water. Also, a fish that is actively feeding is far easier to fool.

You'll often see trout lying motionless, with no flick of the tail and no short forays from their positions. Fish like this are usually napping, spooked, or lethargic from water that's too cold or too warm.

If you've been watching a pool from afar, the longer you look the more trout you'll spot. If you have a choice, look for one or two fish that are plucking food from the drift, with their tails constantly in motion. Start without a strike indicator or weight on the leader. Make sure your leader is at least 12 feet long, preferably 15 feet, and your tippet is at least 4 feet long. The best flies are usually small, drab, and lightly weighted. Pheasant-Tail Nymphs, midge pupae, worm imitations, and scuds are favorite flies for this kind of fishing, but try to match what you see in the water or hatching.

The best approach is to pitch your fly above the fish far enough so it has time to sink to the trout's level. If you are fishing from directly behind it, try to place only the tippet over the fish. If you are fishing off to one side of the fish, try to cast so that nothing falls on its head and only the fly drifts over its position. Placing the fly line over the trout's head is a sure way to send it bolting for deep water. How far ahead of the fish you cast depends on the size and weight of the fly, the water's depth, and the speed of the current. A typical distance in shallow water is three to four feet.

Since it is usually impossible to see your fly in the water, keep your eyes glued on the trout. Often, if you look away for just a few seconds you'll lose sight of the fish or it might move into a place where it's not as easy to spot. Try to gauge when your fly is passing the trout's

These two brown trout feeding in Utah's Green River are perfect opportunities for a carefully presented nymph. Note that their shadows are more distinct than the fish themselves.

position. If the fish moves sideways or lifts off the bottom, gently "pre-strike"—which is a soft but quick movement of either the rod tip or the fly line—to take slack out of the line. Continue to tighten if you feel resistance; if there is no resistance, the trout either refused your fly, moved for something else, or spit it out quickly. At any rate, since you did not rip your line off the water, the fish won't be spooked and sometimes the darting motion will even make the fish chase your fly.

Sometimes you'll see a fish move way off to one side when your fly drifts even with its position. This fish is probably frightened by either your leader or fly—a good sign that you should change position, go to a smaller fly, or add a longer, lighter tippet. Some fish will also get so frightened with your approach that they'll spook and swim away. Some days most of them will. Chuckle or curse and move on.

Signs that a trout is ready to take your fly are a quickening of its tail beats, dropping back in the current, or moving to one side. If you are fishing across from a trout, you might even see a white flash as it opens its mouth. My friend Pat McCord, a Colorado guide and the best sight-fisherman I know, likes to strike just as he sees a fish move back to its original position. They'll invariably do that after eating something, and it avoids a typical problem of striking too soon—when the fish is moving for your fly rather than after it has eaten the fly.

Strike indicators are not very useful when sight fishing; in fact, most times they're a hindrance because they spook the fish and cut down on your casting accuracy. Besides, fish lying in the shallows feeding on nymphs can inhale your fly and spit it out without ever moving the indicator. Many times I've been watching the strike indicator instead of the trout, and when I glance back to the fish I wonder why it's moving its head like a puppy with a rag. By the time I realize the fish is trying to get a piece of metal out of its jaws, it's too late. However, a very tiny piece of yarn, a small dry fly, or a smudge of Strike Putty on the leader can help you gauge the position of the fly. Make sure the indicator is so small that it does not disturb the water when you cast, and keep it at least two feet from the fly. Don't watch the indicator. Use it in your peripheral

Pat McCord sight-fishing to a big trout. You can feel the intensity of his gaze even from this angle.

vision to keep track of the fly's progress, but never take your eyes off the fish.

There will be times when the water is deeper or faster and you'll need a small piece of shot or sink putty on the leader to get your nymph to a trout's level. You'll seldom need weight if you are directly behind a fish, but if you approach them from any sideways angle it's much harder to get the fly down drag-free because the current is yanking on the leader. Keep the weight as small as possible and at least eight inches from the fly. Here, adding two small indicators instead of one helps keep the fly from dragging and lets you approximate its position. Mend softly, keeping both indicators in line and pointing at the fly.

CHAPTER 4

NYMPH WATER

I once had the pleasure of having a whole day on Montana's Bitterroot River when there seemed to be no other anglers or drift boats on the river. I spent the morning fishing the tail of a single pool, catching sturdy wild rainbows and browns on tiny *Trico* mayfly imitations. When the hatch was over and fish stopped rising, I decided to nymph the head of the pool, which I had left untouched all morning. It looked like a per-

Perfect nymph-fishing depth and speed. Joe Bressler thought so, and hooked up on Idaho's South Fork of the Snake.

fect setup for nymphs: a wide, shallow riffle flowing about the speed of a walk and sloping quickly into the depths of the pool. Surface currents were chuckling happily along, with no swirls or sideways currents to ruin a drag-free drift.

If I had taken a beginning fly fisher with me I would have been able to put him into a half-dozen beautiful trout. It was an easy toss into the riffle at the head of the pool, the current sauntering the flies and indicator right over the deep shelf at the head of the pool. I could not find a nymph between Sizes 14 and 20 that the fish would not eat. In a half-hour, I must have taken a dozen browns and rainbows, all over 14 inches with one rainbow over 20. Boy, I thought, I was *hot*. Either that or the river was switched on that day.

Wrong on both counts. After I left this pool, I took only the occasional fish in a mile of water, and none were very large. The pools above looked just as tasty to me, and I'm sure they had nearly as many trout in them—but there was something about the hydraulics of that first pool that made it nymph-fishing Nirvana. I know this because two hours later I fished the exact same spot, this time putting a pinch of sink putty on my tippet and fishing just four feet lower into the pool. Another four or five trout jumped on my nymph, and in a deep pocket on the far side of the riffle I hadn't spotted earlier, a 2-foot brown trout jumped on my Pheasant-Tail Nymph like he hadn't eaten in a week.

In thirty years of fly fishing, this was about the best nymph fishing I ever had, but it had nothing to do with my fly selection and only a little to do with my presentation. I just happened to blunder into the perfect spot at the right time. Not all water in a river holds trout, and not all that holds trout can be fished easily with a nymph. Don't be afraid to experiment, but learn to pick your game on fields where you have the advantage.

RIFFLES AND RUNS

Regardless of whether this water is at the head of a pool or by itself in a long piece of featureless water, if trout live there you'll increase your odds by fishing there. Faster water hides the splash of fly lines and indicators, and the fish have to grab quickly and don't get a good look at our fly. But even more important, riffles are where insects live so trout are more likely to feed here regardless of hatches or water temperatures. Riffles are the fast-food joints in a river; pools are the leisurely dining rooms.

Unless a run's maximum depth is less than three feet, avoid the fastest water. Instead, fish on the edges, or "seams," where fast water meets moderate currents. In a fast run, there is often a perfect slot between the fast water in the middle of the river and the shallow water along the banks. This is usually just beyond the level where you can see bottom, but first make some casts into the shallows. Start with either

Fishing to the deep slot on the edge of a riffle.

no indicator and a direct upstream approach. Unless the current is uniform and without much turbulence, you may need to add a small indicator. As you begin to fish the deeper water, you will need to either add weight or move the indicator toward the fly line. When you get to the deepest part of the run, right at the edge of the main current, it pays to put on more weight and use the high-stick method with or without an indicator.

In long, boring riffles, look for deep slots where the water gets a bit darker. These are especially common along a far bank where they often get overlooked by most anglers. Riffles are often a great spot

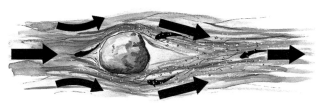

In pocket water, fish one rock at a time. Here's where you'll most often find trout.

for sight-fishing; if you can't spot any trout, try an upstream approach with a lightly weighted nymph, no indicator, and no weight on the leader. Add weight only if you are not ticking the bottom in a dozen casts. And try to keep the indicator in your pocket. Trout in riffles often take the fly with a rush, and it's a good place to learn how to watch the line and leader for strikes.

In turbulent white water with lots of rocks, known as "pocket water," fish the pockets downstream of the rocks, but don't overlook the deep cushions of slower water in front of and along the sides of the rocks. In some rivers, trout strongly prefer the less obvious places in front of rocks. It's essential to fish pocket water with short casts, one rock at a time. A strike indicator is almost a must—the confusing turbulence around the rocks plays havoc with your leader. It's tough enough to figure out where your nymph is drifting, much less if a trout has eaten it. It helps to keep the strike indicator set quite shallow when fishing in pocket water.

HEAD OF A POOL

Since most pools begin as riffles or runs, much that I've said about fast water applies to heads of pools. The main difference is that pools offer a vast haven for trout to hide and rest when danger threatens or when floods or droughts limit safe habitat. Where a deep slot in a riffle might be worth a few dozen casts, the head of a pool may be worth an hour of your time. Because I know

A successful cast to the seam at the head of a pool.

from past experience that I can catch trout easier at the head of a pool, I begin fishing where the fast water first starts to slow and flatten. You'll want to fish all of this water, from the middle of the river to both banks. Even with an indicator and heavy weight, it's difficult to fish the slow water on the far side of a pool without getting instant drag and thus a poor presentation. I can't tell you how many times I've tried to reach my line across the middle of a river without a single hit. Yet as soon as I cross the river and nymph that side from directly below or quartering upstream, my luck changes for the better.

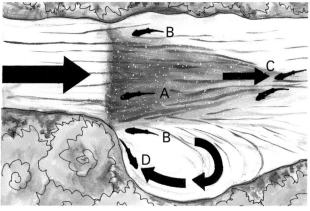

Places to look for trout at the head of a pool. The fish at A is just below the shelf where the pool deepens. The trout at B are in the seam between fast and slow water. The fish at C are in the place where the fast water begins to slow, and the trout at D is in the whirlpool, facing downstream but upcurrent.

Many pools bend to one side at the head. Your best fishing is usually on the inside of the curve. Here, the current is fast enough to provide steady food, yet slow enough so trout can lie in the current without difficulty. Often the inside of the curve will offer one of those beautiful gravel shelves like the one I found on the Bitterroot. Don't pass up the "eye" on either side of the head. Very large trout often move into this shallow water. Be careful, though, as sometimes the eyes are whirlpools, and even when looking upstream the current will be moving toward you. Try to sneak around the bank and fish the whirlpool downstream but up-current.

The best flies for fishing the head of a pool are often larger, meatier patterns, easily spotted by trout in the tumbling water: stonefly nymphs, mayfly imitations, and especially flies with sparkle like Bead-Heads or Flashbacks. Heads of pools are also a source of midge larvae or aquatic worms when the water level rises or the streambed is disturbed by cattle in the water or wading anglers.

MIDDLE AND TAIL OF A POOL

The middle of a pool, where riffles flatten, is a more difficult place to fish nymphs. Look for disturbances in the water where subsurface rocks hold trout, where deep water rolls along a bank, or where downed trees stick out into the pool. In shallow pools, look for the deeper slots where trout feel secure.

The best way to fish the middle of a slow pool is with an indicator large enough to suspend the fly and any weight on the leader.

This is a great place for fishing an unweighted or lightly weighted nymph along a deep bank. Cast a few feet above where you think a trout might lie. Make a Tuck Cast or a slack-line cast so the fly has a chance to sink, then a quick upstream mend. Hold your rod tip at about 45 degrees to keep line off the water, but then let the current have its way with the line. Resist the urge to make any more mends. For some reason, trout in the middle of a pool are more likely to take a nymph when it starts to pull away from the bank and toward the surface. Usually the tip of your floating line will twitch an inch or two when a trout takes the nymph. This does not work well with a strike indicator or weight on the leader— these either spook the fish or prevent the fly from behaving naturally.

The best way I know to fish the middle of a deep pool is to use a yarn indicator large enough to suspend the fly and any weight needed to get the fly close to the bottom. If the water is over three feet deep, you can get away with an indicator the diameter of a silver dollar and will probably need it. In the middle of the pool, things happen in slow motion as compared to a riffle. Although you may not think your indicator is dragging, often the fly line slides the indicator toward you—not enough to create a wake, but enough sideways motion to alert the trout that something is not right. By using a yarn indicator that floats high and suspends the fly, your drift will have some protection from this drag.

Cast upstream and across, and watch the indicator in relation to bubbles or debris on the surface. If it stays in the same lane and follows their progress, you have the right drift. You can even make subtle mends without moving the fly, as the indicator's large mass dampens some movements of the leader. Strikes here often manifest themselves as just a wink of the indicator, as if a tuft of wind has brushed its surface. Set the hook if the indicator even smells like it's going to move. Strikes here may also happen at the end of the drift, so try to lengthen your drift as much as possible.

The tail of a pool makes everything more difficult because the surface current is typically much faster than the current close to the bottom. As soon as you cast, whether you are using a floating line with no indicator or an indicator with a weighted fly and leader, your fly is yanked quickly toward the surface, ruining a drag-free drift. One way to get around this tough situation is to fish downstream, casting plenty of slack and letting the indicator drift until you run out of slack. Another method is to use a Tuck Cast and fish either straight upstream or against the bank.

Don't worry if you have difficulty taking fish from tails of pools with nymphs. Most anglers do. One saving grace of these difficult places is that you sometimes find trout nymphing in shallow water, and with a careful approach you may have some challenging sight fishing. Because trout in the tail of a pool are spooky to the extreme, and because of the difficult current, your best bet is to sneak up behind these fish and cast directly upstream, allowing only the tippet to fall over a trout's head.

CHAPTER 5

A CHANGING GAME

So far we've looked at how immediate physical characteristics of a stream affect nymph fishing. But the game changes on other levels. The variables of weather, season, and time of day add even more complexity—and fun. Even in one pool on a single river, what works today may be useless tomorrow, and you'll see fresh challenges every time you pull on your waders.

EFFECTS OF SEASON

As the season unfolds, water temperatures, water levels, and insect hatches change, sometimes overnight. What worked in April may have to be shelved for the season after May 1, unless you fish a spring creek or tailwater with little fluctuation in water levels and temperatures. This uncertainty is what makes fly fishing so satisfying. Be flexible, study the river, and be ready to change your tackle and presentation every time you put on your fishing vest.

Water Temperature

In general, the further away from the optimum trout water temperatures of 55 to 65 degrees, the more precise you'll have to be with your casting and the closer to the bottom you'll have to get. When trout become active and their metabolic rate is in high gear, they'll often chase your nymph. The following chart may help you determine what flies and techniques to use according to water temperature:

WATER TEMPERATURE	BEST FLIES	TECHNIQUES
Below 40 degrees	Small stoneflies, midge larvae, aquatic worms. Mostly drab patterns tied with weight.	Fish completely dead-drift close to the bottom. Casts must be precise so the fly drifts right in front of where you suspect a fish may be lying. Best fishing in middle of the day.
40 to 50 degrees	All of the above plus mayfly nymph imitations. Bead-Head imitations will also work.	Fish close to the bottom, but trout may move a foot or so for the fly. Best fishing from late afternoon to early evening when water temperatures are increasing.
50 to 65 degrees	Any fly may work, depending on hatches.	All techniques. Fish may be feeding at any level so don't just fish on the bottom. Early morning can be

		spectacular, late morning excellent, middle of the day may not be as easy. Early evening can also be very good, particularly in advance of evening hatches.
65 to 72 degrees	Mostly small patterns like midge larvae, Pheasant-Tails, and tiny caddis pupae. Best flies are size 16 and smaller.	Fish nymphs on a long leader and light tippet in riffles and at heads of pools. Use only a small strike indicator and little weight. Best fishing will be at first light until mid-morning.
Above 72 degrees	None	Don't fish. Trout become too stressed and even playing them quickly can kill them.

Two consecutive days nymphing in cold water can teach you much about water temperature. One April, I fished my first day on Colorado's Roaring Fork on a sunny morning when the water temperature was 40 degrees. I caught some fish on nymphs, but each one was like pulling a stubborn nightcrawler from the ground. By

Even in the coldest water, a rise of a few degrees may put trout on the bite.

A CHANGING GAME

early afternoon, the sun had brought the water up to 42 degrees and I saw a few caddisflies on the water. There were no rises that day, but instead of just inhaling them, the fish began grabbing my nymphs with a vengeance.

The next morning, the water temperature was again 40 degrees when the sun came up, but by 10 A.M. the air temperature was 70 degrees and the water rose to 42 degrees. On this day the fish actively ate my nymphs all morning. By 1 P.M., a strong cold front blew in, clouds obscured the sun, and the water temperature dropped back to 40 degrees. By 5 P.M. it was snowing. Unlike the previous day, when the best fishing was in the afternoon, the action this day stopped at noon like someone had blown a whistle. In the morning I was hooking over a dozen fish an hour; in the entire afternoon I hooked two.

It's not so much absolute water temperature that determines nymphing action; rather, it's the rate of change of the water temperature. Water temperature of 42 degrees is typically thought of as too cold for any kind of trout fishing. Yet that rise of two degrees was enough to switch on every trout in the Roaring Fork. Until water starts to rise out of the prime regime for trout, about 65 degrees, any increase in temperature seems to increase the rate of feeding activity.

Hatches

Hatches always make nymph fishing more productive. When aquatic insects hatch, they are abundant at all levels in the water column, which makes trout more aggressive. Even if you don't have an exact imitation of today's hatch, trout are more likely to take your nymph, but it also pays to get as close as you can. If there are three or four different insects hatching at once, trout may possibly key into one species and ignore the others, but usually they'll feed on anything that drifts near their positions.

It pays to know something about the life cycle of the insect you suspect will hatch today. Turn over a few rocks in the shallows. Insects about to hatch will often be crawling actively under rocks near the bank, and the wing cases on those about to hatch will appear swollen and black. Let's say you arrive on a river early in the morning and see many Size 12 mayfly nymphs in the shallows, rusty brown ones with long tails that look like the March browns you've seen in books. No flies are hatching. You suspect, however, there may be a March brown hatch later in the day.

Fish a March brown imitation close to the bottom, in both deep and shallow water, until you see some flies hatching. If you see flies on the water and spot a few splashy rises, use an unweighted nymph or take weight off the leader and set the strike indicator so the fly rides higher in the water column. If you begin to see more rises, it might pay to take both weight and indicator off the leader and swing your nymph over the fish. And if you see fish actually taking flies off the surface, get rid of that nymph and have some fun with a dry fly. From a practical standpoint, at the height of a heavy hatch, there are more empty nymph shucks in the water than juicy full ones. I suspect trout figure this out, and may eat only floating flies during bountiful hatches.

WATER LEVEL

Typically, high and fast water happens in the early season when water temperatures are cold and trout are sluggish. This presents you with a double whammy—in the cold water you must fish your nymph perfectly dead drift and close to the bottom, but fast currents and deep water make that presentation exasperating. Nymph fishing gets better when the water drops because it's easier to get your fly to the fish, and when water temperatures rise because they will move farther for a piece of food.

A rise of water with temperatures closer to the optimum, after a quick rainstorm or when water is released from a dam, presents a productive opportunity followed by disappointment. When water levels first rise, insects, crustaceans, and aquatic worms get washed into the current and trout take advantage of the bounty, feeding heavily and aggressively. Provided you find the right fly and presentation, fishing should be rewarding. However, after a few hours or as long as a day, the feeding rate decreases. Some say the trout get "fed up" and aren't hungry anymore. I suspect, however, that the water eventually gets so full of debris that trout have trouble discerning between food and bits of inedible matter, and the water may also get so dirty that they can't find any food. When this happens, a fly fished with subtle drag, swung across the current so that it stands out from the debris, may be productive.

When water levels drop to the point that those previously good places to fish are either dry or too shallow, nymph fishing stays productive—it may just get tougher. In contrast to rising water, where all sorts of edible goodies are drifting by, low water offers food only when insects are hatching. Insects that hatch during low water are usually small, so you'll have to go to a smaller fly—perhaps one that represents the immature stage of the hatch of the day. Also, trout get spookier and harder to approach as the water drops, so use a lighter leader, a longer tippet, little or no weight on the leader, and smaller strike indicators. A happy up-side to very low water is that sight-fishing is better because the trout are easier to spot.

TIME OF DAY

Time of day strongly affects water temperature, but there are other aspects of daily changes in light levels, independent of water temperature, that present opportunities for nymph fishing. It's often said trout don't like to feed in bright sunlight. However, behavioral studies of trout, and my own experiences, don't substantiate this. Trout get spookier with bright overhead light, and many insects don't hatch as readily. But trout continue to feed, and you'll catch them if you go

Early morning, before the sun hits the water, is often the best time to fish a nymph.

to a light fly line (4-weight or under), a long leader (12 feet or better), and subtle weight with tiny strike indicators. Stick to riffled water during the day as well.

Diurnal drift is a behavioral trait of insects related to light levels that changes little with temperature or abundance of hatches. After the sun goes down each day, many insects crawl out from under their rocks and release their purchase on the bottom, drifting a few feet or hundreds of yards under the cover of darkness. It's an adaptive measure designed to recolonize a river and to avoid overpopulation, as most insects fly upstream when hatching, forming mating flights and laying eggs. Insects have adapted this behavior to hours of darkness to avoid predators. Trout can see at night but probably not well enough to feed on small objects drifting below the surface. At first light, however, many insects are finishing their drift and settling down in their new homes, and trout can see well enough to pluck them from the drift. For a few hours each morning, nymph fishing is amazingly productive, yet most angler miss out because they are looking for hatches or other signs of feeding activity. You won't see anything either, but if you drag your butt out of bed you'll have the best nymph fishing you've ever seen. Obviously water temperatures must be high enough that trout are active, so this activity peaks in late spring or early summer when overnight temperatures don't drop below 55 degrees, and it's over by the time the sun strikes the water.

The other idiosyncrasy of nymph fishing related to daylight, or lack of it, is evening fishing. I've noticed that, even if insect hatches are abundant, nymphing success declines between sunset and dark. This is the time when insects are often on the surface, but even on days with no hatches you'll get fewer takes to your nymphs as it gets darker. Why? It finally made sense to me one evening on Colorado's Blue River. I switched from a nymph with weight and a strike indicator to an unweighted Hare's-Ear Nymph fished ten inches below a Stimulator dry fly. Nothing was hatching and nothing touched the dry, but several very respectable browns and rainbows grabbed the nymph. It suddenly occurred to me that trout couldn't *see* my nymph fished close to the bottom, but when it was fished close to the surface, it showed up like a beacon, silhouetted against the fading skylight.

This might be obvious to you, but after 40 years of fly fishing it was a revelation to me. I'm a little slow. I hope you enjoy similar bolts from the blue as you encounter the world of nymph fishing.

INDEX